WITTGENSTEIN
and Modern Philosophy

Born in Denmark in 1912, **Justus Hartnack**, after having served in the Danish Army as an officer, received the M.A. in philosophy in 1946 and the Ph.D. in 1950 from the University of Copenhagen. From 1946 to 1954 he was in the United States on the faculty of Colgate University; he then returned to Denmark to become chairman of the philosophy department at Aarhus University, a position he held until 1972. He has served as visiting professor at Vassar College and at New York University. His last post was as a distinguished professor at the State University of New York at Brockport. His publications include books on Kant, Hegel, the history of philosophy, and human rights. He is now an emeritus from both Aarhus University and the State University of New York and lives in Oxford, England, and Helsingør, Denmark.

Born in London in 1920, **Maurice Cranston** was educated at Oxford, where he wrote a thesis on the freedom of the will. At the present time, Mr. Cranston is a Reader in Political Science at the London School of Economics. He has contributed many articles to various literary and philosophical journals, and is the author of *Freedom, What Are Human Rights?, Jean-Paul Sartre,* and the standard biography of John Locke.

WITTGENSTEIN

and Modern Philosophy

BY JUSTUS HARTNACK

SECOND EDITION

Translated by Maurice Cranston

UNIVERSITY OF NOTRE DAME PRESS
NOTRE DAME, INDIANA 46556

Wittengenstien and Modern Philosophy was originally published
in Danish by Gyldendal, Copenhagen, in 1962 under the title
Wittgenstien Og Den Moderne Filosofi.
© 1962 Justus Hartnack
Translation Copyright © 1965 by Methuen & Co. Ltd.
First published in the U.S. by Anchor Books, 1965

Second Edition © 1986 by
University of Notre Dame
Notre Dame, Indiana 46556
http://www.undpress.nd.edu
Printed by Arrangement with the Author
All Rights Reserved

Reprinted in 2002

Manufactured in the United States of America

Library of Congress Cataloging-in-Publication Data
Hartnack, Justus.
    Wittgenstein and modern philosophy.

    Translation of: Wittgenstein og den moderne filosofi.
    1. Wittgenstein, Ludwig, 1889–1951.   I. Title.
B3376.W564H3313   1985   192   85-40604
ISBN 0-268-01936-3
ISBN 0-268-01937-1 (pbk.)

∞*This book is printed on acid-free paper.*

Reader's adviser 14th ed. 1994

CONTENTS

PREFACE

Twentieth-century philosophy, more than that of any other period, has become deeply and sharply conscious of the connection between philosophical problems and language. No one has contributed more to this new awareness than Ludwig Wittgenstein, who died in 1951. To understand the connection between philosophy and language is to understand Wittgenstein; without understanding that, one cannot understand him. And precisely because Wittgenstein holds the key to modern philosophical activity, there is an obvious need for an exposition of his thought.

But however keenly it may be felt, that need is not one that can be easily met. For what Wittgenstein says in his very personal and often aphoristic way cannot simply be restated; it must be interpreted, and interpretations, as often as not, are controversial.

We now seem to have entered what might well be called the Wittgensteinian moment in philosophy. Books about his work are becoming more numerous, and interest in his thought is becoming more widespread. The moment dates from the publication in 1922 of his first book, *Tractatus Logico-Philosophicus*, followed by the posthumous publication in 1953 of the work of his later years, *Philosophical Investigations*. In the pages which follow, I have tried to give a general survey of Wittgenstein's thought, considering both the *Tractatus* and the *Philosophical Investigations*, and also to give some account of the influence which these two very different books have exercised. My essay is thus to some extent an account of what is not altogether correctly known as "analytical philosophy." In my last chapter I have hinted—but done no more than hint—at something I believe to be of great importance, namely that Wittgenstein's later philosophy can throw light on a very wide and diverse range of problems.

PREFACE TO THE SECOND EDITION

The original Danish edition of *Wittgenstein and Modern Philosophy (Wittgenstein Og Den Moderne Filosofi)* was first published in 1962, after the manuscript was completed in 1959. For whatever reasons, the book enjoyed great success, if not in Denmark, at least in some other countries (in fact, in seven other countries besides Denmark and by nine different publishers). One reason, I suppose, is this: the book was published at the time when the popularity of Wittgenstein had its beginnings. Many, therefore, wanted a book which in a relatively clear and concise way could serve as an introduction to his thought, and do it without compromising his position.

Needless to say, during a quarter of a century—during which Wittgensteinian scholarship seems to have reached its peak—many of the problems dealt with by Wittgensteinians have received a deeper analysis than they did in this book.

My book describes and analyzes Wittgenstein's thought as presented in the then only published works: *Tractatus Logico-Philosophicus,* first published in 1922, and the *Philosophical Investigations,* published posthumously in 1953.

After I had finished my manuscript, the *Blue Book*

and the *Brown Book* were published. Both were originally manuscripts Wittgenstein dictated as notes to his students, the *Blue Book* in 1933–1934 and the *Brown Book*, which may be regarded as a first draft of the *Philosophical Investigations,* during the following year. The *Blue Book* and the *Brown Book* were therefore neither described nor analyzed in my book. But even if they had been published before 1958, to include an analysis of them would have meant a digression from the intent and purpose of my book. Such a coverage would surely have had historical interest, but for the purpose of acquiring a knowledge and an understanding of Wittgenstein's philosophy, of his message and his contribution to philosophy, it is, so I think, the *Tractatus* and the *Philosophical Investigations* that are important. And this judgment is not altered, I believe, by the many manuscripts which Wittgenstein left behind him and which now, by and large, have been published.

A philosopher as great and at the same time as difficult as Wittgenstein has been the subject of innumerable studies, and universal agreement on how to interpret him cannot be expected. This is true of almost all great thinkers, past and present. This is why we still benefit from studies of Plato, Aristotle, Descrates, Spinoza, Kant, or Hegel, to mention just a few. New studies and scholarly works on Wittgenstein will continue to appear. I do think, however, that a reliable brief orientation to his thought is, if not essential, then at least a very useful way to begin a study of his philosophy.

The intense interest in the philosophy of Wittgenstein probably has reached its peak, to decline in coming years. But one thing seems to be certain. The impact Wittgenstein has made on philosophy will remain. Just as we cannot philosophize today as we did before Berkeley and Hume, or as we did before Kant or Hegel, so we cannot philosophize today as we did before the

Tractatus and the *Philosophical Investigations.* We may be ignorant about the details of the thought and arguments of the great philosophers of the past; nevertheless the impact of that which made them great is almost ineradicably implanted in our way of thinking.

I

Biographical Introduction

Who was Wittgenstein? It is no easy matter to answer this question, for Wittgenstein is still so close to us, still so much a figure of our own time, still so much talked about, exalted and denounced, that an objective and balanced appraisal is difficult to achieve. Posterity must determine his exact place in the history of philosophy; but at any rate there can be no doubt that he was a genius. This is not to say that he was the only genius, or even the greatest genius, in twentieth-century philosophy; indeed, it scarcely matters whether he was or was not. What does matter is that Wittgenstein's work in philosophy was passionate, intense, inspired. He dedicated himself to it; philosophy was his

3

life. Every train of thought that he might have followed with greater zeal, every problem that he might have worked on with a fiercer determination, was not, for him, something that he might have done better, it was a betrayal of his real mission in life, treason against his own existence, a *sin*. Such total commitment to philosophy allows us to compare Wittgenstein with the greatest names in the history of the subject; what was characteristic of Socrates and Spinoza was characteristic also of him.

Because his whole being was so consumed with passionate thought, Wittgenstein could not give lectures as other university teachers do. To lecture in the ordinary way is to expound, or repeat what has already been thought; and to repeat a thought is not to think it, at any rate, not to think it with Wittgenstein's kind of intensity. So instead of giving conventional lectures, Wittgenstein *thought* what he said as he spoke. He did not reproduce what he had prepared before. And it was precisely because he went through this process of thinking in such a fresh, powerful and concentrated way, in the presence of his students, that he earned their respect, and even something approaching veneration.

Of course his lectures were not elegant in style or form; they were a kind of research, which really serious students—and only such attended Wittgenstein's lectures—found strangely inspiring. For them it was like being in the workshop of a great master where they could witness, and perhaps even participate in, the creation of new and often exhilarating thoughts.

A professor has his students and, if he is the founder of a school, his followers. Wittgenstein had both, but he also had disciples. It was perhaps not difficult to become his disciple because of his magnetic and compelling personality and because of the originality and depth and fervor of his thought. Wittgenstein was conscious of this, and regretted it. A disciple's spiritual dependence on his master at best hinders independent thought, and, at worst, prevents it. And a thought which is not independent is a thought only half understood. It contains no personal truth.

This is the dilemma of anyone who wishes to transmit knowledge and learning to others. On the one hand, to teach is to pass on your own knowledge to the pupil, to introject your own knowledge into him. On the other hand, learning is not mere receiving. For knowledge is not knowledge if it is without insight and understanding; both must be there if anything is learned, and neither can be received like a gift. Wittgenstein's belief recalls that of Plato, who, in the *Menon*, likens the teacher's role to that of the midwife. To teach is not to instill a true idea in the pupil, but to help him to think it himself.

Among those called Wittgenstein's disciples were several who have proved themselves to be original and gifted thinkers. Several of the leading philosophers of the present generation, not only in England and America, but even in places like Finland, are men who studied under Wittgenstein. Admission to his lectures was always restricted; he would receive only those students who would undertake to attend regularly for at least one term. He insisted that his lectures were not for tourists, but only for students who took philosophy seriously and would apply themselves to the study of its problems with something like his own devotion. There were never more than fifteen students at his lectures, but most of the men who heard them were marked by them indelibly.

Wittgenstein was not at all English, either by birth or temperament, but as an Austrian Jew, living and working in England, he became a British subject after

Hitler's annexation of Austria. He was born in Vienna in 1889, the son of a rich engineer. After studying for two years at the School of Engineering in Berlin, he went to the University of Manchester in 1908. His interest soon passed from engineering to mathematics, and from mathematics to the principles of mathematics. So he left Manchester for Cambridge, to study under the then leading British logician, Bertrand Russell, coauthor with Whitehead of *Principia Mathematica*, a revolutionary work on the history of logic and mathematics.

From 1911 to 1913 Wittgenstein remained in Cambridge. Then, in order to think and work in solitude, he went to live in a primitive dwelling near Bergen, Norway. At the outbreak of the first World War he enlisted in the Austrian army, was trained to be an officer, but was taken prisoner by the Italians at the time of the Austrian debacle. His first published work appeared in an Austrian periodical, *Annalen der Naturphilosophie*, in 1921, and was published in book form in London in 1922 with the title *Tractatus Logico-Philosophicus*. In this book there is an introduction by Russell, and also a translation into English, printed on the right-hand pages opposite Wittgenstein's own text on the left-hand pages. Wittgenstein's work is difficult to translate, and he felt that the English rendering did not correspond to what he was saying in German. He was not satisfied either with this translation of the *Tractatus* or with Russell's introduction.

The *Tractatus* is written in an almost aphoristic form, and its meaning is elusive. There is no general agreement as to how it should be read. Nevertheless, it has had an enormous influence among philosophers. Its influence was particularly marked on the logical positivism that became so fashionable in the years be-

6

tween the wars. Later, interest in the *Tractatus* diminished a little, chiefly because Wittgenstein himself repudiated its central ideas and developed a new approach to the basic problems of philosophy. More recently, however, there has been a renewal of interest in the *Tractatus*, partly because of the light which was thrown on the author's intentions by the manuscripts and notes which were found after his death, and partly because of the contrast between the *Tractatus* and Wittgenstein's later teaching. I shall return to this question in another chapter of this essay.

On the death of his father in 1912, Wittgenstein inherited a considerable fortune, but he promptly gave this away and earned his living in miscellaneous jobs; at one time he was a village schoolmaster in Austria, at another, a gardener in a monastery. However, in 1929 some Cambridge philosophers persuaded him to return to that university, where he became a Fellow of Trinity College. Ten years later, on the retirement of G. E. Moore, he was elected to one of the professorial chairs in philosophy, but the second World War broke out before he could take up his duties. Wittgenstein found war-work as an orderly in a London hospital, and later worked in a medical laboratory in Newcastle. Before the end of the war he had returned to Cambridge, but in 1947 he resigned his chair at the age of 58.

Wittgenstein disliked, indeed loathed, being a Cambridge don, not only because academic duties were boring and took up too much time, but for a moral reason. He believed that being a professor jeopardized the intellectual integrity of a philosopher. It is not easy to say why he took this stern view. Certain passages in his published writings confirm it, but none that I know of explains it. Conceivably Wittgenstein felt that a man is a genuine philosopher only when his mind is tormented by problems, so that his whole being must be concentrated on their solution. His efforts to solve them are in a sense efforts to safeguard his existence. The effort required for teaching is quite different. To teach philosophy is not to philosophize; thus a philosopher who teaches is, as a teacher, no philosopher. I must emphasize that this is only a conjecture, and quite possibly wrong. The fact remains, however, that Wittgenstein did have a moral objection to being a professor, and he left Cambridge in 1947. Afterward he lived for a time in solitude in a cottage on the west coast of Ireland, and later stayed at a hotel in Dublin. Then he was found to be suffering from cancer, and in 1949 he went back to live in Cambridge. He died there on April 29, 1951, three days after his sixty-second birthday.

The lectures he gave at Cambridge in the 1930's revealed a break with the ideas put forward in the *Tractatus*. Among the manuscripts he left at his death was one *Philosophische Untersuchungen*, which was later published as *Philosophical Investigations*, with, once more, Wittgenstein's German text on the left-hand pages and the English translation on the right-hand pages. In essentials this book marks a new beginning. For this reason Wittgenstein occupies a singular place in the history of philosophy, having first at an early age written a work which exercised a decisive influence on the philosophical thought of his time, and then, in his mature years, rejecting his early theory and producing a second theory which, for sheer originality, stature and influence, is even more important than the first. Many philosophers have enriched the subject with more than one theory. Some have progressed from one point of view to another, so that a line of development can be traced in their work. But what makes Wittgenstein unique is that he has produced two entirely distinct and original philosophical works of genius.

8

Apart from the *Philosophical Investigations*, the chief posthumously published works of Wittgenstein are *Remarks on the Foundations of Mathematics* (1956), printed like the others with an English translation opposite the author's German text, and a work in English called *The Blue and Brown Books* (1958). These last were composed of notes dictated by Wittgenstein, the *Blue Book* in 1933–34, the *Brown Book* in 1934–35. They were dictated, that is to say, after Wittgenstein had rejected the theory put forward in the *Tractatus* but before he had reached the standpoint elaborated in the *Philosophical Investigations*. It is worth noting that the editor of *The Blue and Brown Books* has given it the subtitle *Preliminary Studies for the Philosophical Investigations*. This latter work was probably begun in 1936 and finished in 1949.

Little has been published about Wittgenstein's life and personality, but one book which can be recommended is *Ludwig Wittgenstein: A Memoir* by Norman Malcolm, which also contains a biographical sketch by Georg Henrik Von Wright. Von Wright, a Finn, was a pupil of Wittgenstein—his only Scandinavian pupil—and he appears to have been able to enter the world of his teacher's ideas more successfully than others. When Wittgenstein resigned his chair at Cambridge, Von Wright was elected to succeed him, but he, in turn, resigned after a few years and became a professor in Helsinki. Von Wright's sketch of Wittgenstein is very readable as well as objective and reliable; and the longer memoir by the American professor, Norman Malcolm, another pupil of Wittgenstein, is also written with tact and skill.

II

The *Tractatus Logico-Philosophicus*

1

Language, according to one traditional notion, consists of words and each word possesses meaning insofar as it stands for something. One learns a language, in this view, by learning what each word refers to; words are names, and to know a language is to know what all the words denote. Hence a word which does not denote anything would not be a word at all; it would be a mere sound; it would be meaningless.

Several philosophers have built theories on such a view of language. The great Scottish philosopher David Hume (1711–76) was one who held that only those words which stand for objects have meaning.[1] On the basis of this theory of language, Hume claimed that such words as "soul," "self" and "power" are meaningless. We have never observed, nor shall we ever be able to observe, anything that could be called a soul, a self or a power; hence those words have no meaning. Even so, the notion that words are names was not supposed to apply to all words. Words like "dog," "table," "tree" were said to be names; but not words which function as "logical constants," that is to say, words like "not," "and," "if," "or." It was not felt to be a problem that such words could not be held in any sense to be names. But there were other cases where considerable logical expertness was needed to sustain the notion that words were names.

If I say that the upper book to the left is red, then it might seem obvious that "the upper book to the left" refers to or names that particular book, and what is being said about that particular book is that it is red. This is summed up by saying that the words "the upper book to the left" is the subject, and the words "is red" is the predicate. But suppose I say "The round square does not exist"? Can we say now that the expression "the round square" is the subject? Can we say that the words "the round square" *name* the round square? Or more precisely, can we say this and at the same time say that no such object as the round square

[1] Hume's terminology, however, is not always clear. Sometimes he speaks of objects, but more often of "impressions"—i.e. sense data. Whatever is felt, seen, heard, smelled or tasted is a sense impression or sense datum. In *Enquiries* (Sect. II, ed. Selby-Bigge, Second Ed., 1927, p.22) Hume writes: "When we entertain, therefore, any suspicion that a philosophical term is employed without any meaning or idea (as is but too frequent), we need but enquire, *from what impression is that supposed idea derived?* And if it be impossible to assign any, this will serve to confirm our suspicion."

exists? What does not exist cannot very well be named. To name is to name *something,* and when there is no "something," there is nothing to name.

Only two ways out of this dilemma seem possible. First, we might follow the German philosopher Meinong[2] and claim that since the expression "the round square" must refer to something, there must at least be a conceptual entity which bears the name and to which the expression refers. Alternatively, it could be argued that the expression "the round square" neither refers to nor names anything. But if this way is chosen, it seems to entail—does it not?—the rejection of the notion that all words save logical constants are names, and with it the notion that the meaning of a word is what it stands for. No one can deny that the statement "The round square does not exist" is true; thus no one can claim that the expression "the round square" is without meaning, for if it had no meaning, the statement could be neither true nor false. It follows the expression "the round square" means something, but names nothing.

It was only thanks to Russell's brilliant solution[3] to this problem that the name-theory of language survived. The expression "the round square" is not a subject at all, and there is no need to invoke, with Meinong, a mystical entity. The statement "The round square does not exist" has, in truth, no subject whatever. Its grammatical form is such that it leads one to believe that it has a subject—i.e. the round square—but it is the aim of philosophical analysis to find the correct, or logical, form of this statement. Now what

[2] A. Meinong (1853–1920). See his *Über Gegenstandstheorie* (p.9): "The lover of paradoxical utterance might very well say: 'Objects do not exist of which it is said that such objects do not exist.'" (trans.)

[3] See his article "On Denoting" in *Mind,* 1905.

the statement actually says is that there is no subject, no subject about which it would be possible to predicate that it was both round and square. Thus restated, the assertion contains only words that *do* name, or refer to, existing things, namely the properties round and square. What the statement says is that both these properties cannot be predicated about one and the same object.

Thus, according to Russell, the grammatical form of the statement "The round square does not exist" misleads us into thinking that it has the same logical form, and this leads to more or less absurd metaphysical conjectures. What is needed is a reformulation of the statement in such a way that its grammatical form gives a true image of its logical form. It is the task of philosophical analysis to reveal the logical form. According to Russell, the logical form of the statement "The round square does not exist" is "There is no entity which is both round and square." For the sake of completeness, it should be added that he gave the statement the following final form: "It is not true that there is an entity c such that the propositional function 'x is square and round' is true, if x is c and otherwise false."[4]

If the logical form of statement is commonly distorted in everyday language, then there would seem to be an urgent need to construct a language in which the logical form is preserved. Such indeed was Russell's own conclusion.[5] But it was not Wittgenstein's. He did not think there was any need to construct a new language because he held that there is only one language. From a logical point of view, all languages are

---

[4] This needs to be modified. For Russell held that a proposition was not accurately expressed unless it was in the symbolic language of *Principia Mathematica*. (Intro., Chap. III, p.66.)
[5] See Russell's remarks in *My Philosophical Development*, p.165.

one language, one language with respect to the logical conditions they must satisfy. And it was these conditions that were of interest to Wittgenstein.

2

In the *Tractatus* Wittgenstein argues that language is a picture of reality. This means there must be a similarity of structure between that which pictures and that which is pictured. The form of language must be the same as that of reality. If the structure is distorted, the result will be nonsense. In other words, it is possible to formulate meaningful statements only if the form of the language is in accordance with the structure of reality. This helps to explain Wittgenstein's remark in the preface to the *Tractatus:* "The whole sense of the book might be summed up in the following words: what can be said at all can be said clearly and what we cannot talk about we must consign to silence."[6] And equally his remarks toward the end of the book: "When the answer cannot be put into words, neither can the question be put into words. The *riddle* does not exist. If a question can be framed at all, it is possible to answer it."[7] Or again: "Skepticism is *not* irrefutable, but obviously nonsensical, when it tries to raise doubts where no questions can be asked. For doubt can exist only when a question exists, a question only when an answer exists and an answer only where something *can be said.*"[8]

In the *Tractatus*, Wittgenstein sets out seven propositions. To each he assigns a number, so that the first

[6] *Tractatus*, p.3. (All quotations from this work are taken from the new translation by O. F. Pears and B. F. McGuinness; Routledge and Kegan Paul, London, 1961.)
[7] Ibid. 6.5 (p.149).
[8] Ibid. 6.51 (p.149).

is 1, the second 2, and so on. Each proposition, except the last, is followed by various comments. The comments on proposition 1 are numbered 1.1 and 1.2; on proposition 2 they are 2.1 and 2.2. But there are also comments on the comments, each numbered on the same principle, so that comments to 1.1 are numbered 1.11 and 1.12, comments to 3.2 are numbered 3.21, 3.22, 3.23, and so on.

The first proposition reads: "The world is all that is the case."[9] That which is the case he calls *facts* (*Tatsachen*). Therefore "the world is the totality of facts, not of things."[10] There is a difference between a thing (or an object) and a fact. A thing is bound up with the notion of a fact but it is not itself a fact. It is a fact that my watch is lying on the table, but neither the watch nor the table is a fact. The watch is a thing and the table is a thing, whereas it is a fact that my watch is lying on the table. This is what is meant by saying that the world consists of facts and not things.

Now we come to a new expression. In his second proposition, Wittgenstein says: "What is the case—a fact—is the existence of states of affairs."[11] A "state of affairs" is a fact that in itself does not consist of facts. Though it is a fact that I have been in Edinburgh and in London, this does not make a state of affairs, but only two facts, that I have been in Edinburgh and that I have been in London. A state of affairs is a combination of things; and a thing is a simple, an irreducible entity, or what Wittgenstein calls substance. But things in this sense must not be identified with ordinary objects like tables, stones, animals and plants. In Wittgenstein's view such objects are complex objects,

[9] Ibid. 1 (p.7).
[10] Ibid. 1.1 (p.7).
[11] Ibid. 2 (p.7).

18

made up of objects which are perhaps complex themselves, but reducible ultimately to simple irreducible objects.

3

We have now been led to the following position: the world consists of states of affairs (and not objects). Objects are the constituents, so that changes in the combination of objects govern changes in the states of affairs.

We come next to language. Language is a picture or model of the facts.[12] Language, in other words, is not a picture of objects but of the combination of objects that constitute a fact. An object can be named, but to name is not to picture. To describe an object would in a sense not be to describe an object at all, but to picture a fact. Suppose there is an object O. A description might state that it is, for example, red. But that O is red is a fact. This leads to the conclusion that objects can only be named. We have only two choices: either to name an object or picture a fact. More precisely, objects must be named for facts to be pictured.[13]

[12] "We picture facts to ourselves." Ibid. 2.1 (p.15); "A picture is a model of reality." Ibid. 2.12 (p.15).
[13] I think that Wittgenstein does not distinguish clearly here between the logical and ontological perspective. A substance can be that about which something is predicated in a given statement. The logical subject of a proposition names the thing (or substance), and in this particular context it is therefore simple. Both "Denmark" in the statement "Denmark is a kingdom" and "this stone" in the statement "This stone is heavy" are substances. In other contexts, they need not be. The object as such is neither one nor the other. Yet Wittgenstein also speaks as if he considered the substances as the essential and in all respects the simple objects of the world, in which case neither "Denmark" nor "this stone" could in any way qualify as substances. But as Wittgenstein says very little on this question, I may well have misunderstood him.

Language consists of sentences, and sentences picturing a state of affairs are elementary sentences. To say that an elementary sentence is a model or picture of a state of affairs is to say, among other things, that a state of affairs exists. Thus every sentence becomes a *proposition*—that is, a sentence by means of which one asserts that something is or is not the case. If an elementary sentence, or, better, an elementary proposition is true, then the state of affairs which is spoken of exists; if the proposition is false, it does not exist.

To claim that language consists only of propositions is to put a radical limitation on what language can do, and Wittgenstein came in his later work to reject this limitation. Even so, such a limitation is bound to follow from the analysis of language as a picture of facts.[14] Another point worth noticing is that one elementary proposition cannot contradict another elementary proposition.[15] Unfortunately Wittgenstein provides no actual example of an elementary proposition. One of the reasons for this may be that no sentence taken from ordinary language satisfies the demands that must be met for it to qualify as an elementary proposition. These demands are certainly very exacting. Behind these demands may lie the fol-

[14] "The simplest kind of proposition, an elementary proposition, asserts the existence of a state of affairs." *Tractatus* 4.21 (p.59); and again: "The sense of a proposition is its agreement and disagreement with possibilities of existence and nonexistence of states of affairs." Ibid. 4.2 (p.59).

[15] Ibid. 4.211 (p.59). Thus Wittgenstein writes: "It is clear that the logical product of two elementary propositions can be neither a tautology nor a contradiction." (6.3751, p.145) The logical product of two propositions is a proposition formed by asserting both of them. The logical product of the proposition "It is raining" and the proposition "It is cold" is the proposition that "It is raining and cold." A tautology is a proposition that cannot be other than true, e.g. "It is either snowing or not snowing."

READ TO THE RHYTHM!

lowing choice: one might hold that the world is as it is because it is logically necessary, because it could not be imagined to be otherwise than as it is; or, alternatively, one might hold that the world is *not* necessarily what it is, but something contingent, a fact based on experiences and not logical necessity. Wittgenstein takes the second view. He also holds that the constituent elements of the world, what he calls "states of affairs," are logically independent of one another.[16] It follows from this that the corresponding true elementary propositions are also logically independent of one another. Hence, as Wittgenstein himself pointed out,[17] a proposition that denies an elementary proposition is not itself an elementary proposition.

4

We come now to a crucial point. What is it about a picture of a fact that makes it a *picture* of one? Ordinarily, when we speak of a picture we mean something which has some resemblance to what it depicts. What is meant by saying that something "resembles" something else is clear enough in the case of drawings and paintings and statues. A painting resembles (or does not resemble) the person (or the landscape) it is supposed to depict. But how can a proposition resemble a fact? A fact has no appearance. A painting may be square and blue and white, but the fact that it is square and blue and white is neither square nor blue and white. To suggest that it were would be to talk nonsense.

[16] "States of affairs are independent of one another." Ibid. 2.061 (p.13). Again: "From the existence or nonexistence of one state of affairs, it is impossible to infer the existence or nonexistence of another." Ibid. 2.062 (p.13).
[17] Vide G. E. M. Anscombe, *An Introduction to Wittgenstein's Tractatus*, p.34.

A state of affairs, we have seen, is a
objects. The picture of a state of affair
tion of names. Every object has a corre
and every name a corresponding object
ignates. A statement's being a picture
affairs has nothing to do with the sp
nunciation of the names, but it has so
with the way those names are put toget
is characterized by the objects being
certain manner, and a sentence is chara
names of the objects being combined in
ner. In other words, what makes the li
a picture of what it depicts is the similar
The combination of names in a senten
it a picture (either true or false) of th
the *logical form* of the sentence.[19] The
the fact have a similar logical form, or
the logical form of the statement and t
of the fact are identical.[20]

What determines the logical form
logical form which is repeated, so to sp
tence)? It is determined by the kinds o

[18] "The fact that the elements of a picture are
other in a determinate way represents that th
one another in the same way." *Tractatus* 2.1
[19] "What any picture, of whatever form, must
with reality, in order to be able to depict it
rectly—in any way at all, is logical form, i.e. th
Ibid. 2.18 (p.17).
[20] "There must be something identical in a pi
depicts, to enable the one to be a picture of
Ibid. 2.161 (p.15). Compare the following: "
ord, the musical idea, the written notes and th
stand to one another in the same internal rel
that holds between language and the world.
structed according to a common logical pla
youths in the fairy tale, their two houses and tl
all in a certain sense one.)" Ibid. 4.014 (p. 3

lowing choice: one might hold that the world is as it is because it is logically necessary, because it could not be imagined to be otherwise than as it is; or, alternatively, one might hold that the world is *not* necessarily what it is, but something contingent, a fact based on experiences and not logical necessity. Wittgenstein takes the second view. He also holds that the constituent elements of the world, what he calls "states of affairs," are logically independent of one another.[16] It follows from this that the corresponding true elementary propositions are also logically independent of one another. Hence, as Wittgenstein himself pointed out,[17] a proposition that denies an elementary proposition is not itself an elementary proposition.

4

We come now to a crucial point. What is it about a picture of a fact that makes it a *picture* of one? Ordinarily, when we speak of a picture we mean something which has some resemblance to what it depicts. What is meant by saying that something "resembles" something else is clear enough in the case of drawings and paintings and statues. A painting resembles (or does not resemble) the person (or the landscape) it is supposed to depict. But how can a proposition resemble a fact? A fact has no appearance. A painting may be square and blue and white, but the fact that it is square and blue and white is neither square nor blue and white. To suggest that it were would be to talk nonsense.

[16] "States of affairs are independent of one another." Ibid. 2.061 (p.13). Again: "From the existence or nonexistence of one state of affairs, it is impossible to infer the existence or nonexistence of another." Ibid. 2.062 (p.13).
[17] Vide G. E. M. Anscombe, *An Introduction to Wittgenstein's Tractatus*, p.34.

A state of affairs, we have seen, is a combination of objects. The picture of a state of affairs is a combination of names. Every object has a corresponding name and every name a corresponding object, which it designates. A statement's being a picture of a state of affairs has nothing to do with the spelling and pronunciation of the names, but it has something to do with the way those names are put together.[18] The fact is characterized by the objects being combined in a certain manner, and a sentence is characterized by the names of the objects being combined in a certain manner. In other words, what makes the linguistic picture a picture of what it depicts is the similarity of structure. The combination of names in a sentence which makes it a picture (either true or false) of the fact is called the *logical form* of the sentence.[19] The statement and the fact have a similar logical form, or, more exactly, the logical form of the statement and the logical form of the fact are identical.[20]

What determines the logical form of a fact (the logical form which is repeated, so to speak, in the sentence)? It is determined by the kinds of objects which

[18] "The fact that the elements of a picture are related to one another in a determinate way represents that things are related to one another in the same way." *Tractatus* 2.15 (p.15).

[19] "What any picture, of whatever form, must have in common with reality, in order to be able to depict it—correctly or incorrectly—in any way at all, is logical form, i.e. the form of reality." Ibid. 2.18 (p.17).

[20] "There must be something identical in a picture and what it depicts, to enable the one to be a picture of the other at all." Ibid. 2.161 (p.15). Compare the following: "a gramophone record, the musical idea, the written notes and the sound waves, all stand to one another in the same internal relation of depicting that holds between language and the world. They are all constructed according to a common logical plan. (Like the two youths in the fairy tale, their two houses and their lilies. They are all in a certain sense one.)" Ibid. 4.014 (p.39).

22

constitute the fact. Different kinds of facts are made possible by different kinds of objects. The nature of the object governs the state of affairs in which it may be found.[21] This does not mean that to know the object is to know what is the case, what states of affairs are true, or, what comes to the same thing, which elementary propositions are true.

The nature of the object, or what Wittgenstein also calls the form of the object, only tells us what is possible; it tells us nothing about what is actually true.[22] In other words, a picture is still a picture whether it depicts a truly existing fact or only a possible fact. The words "possible fact" do not mean something that may *possibly* be the case (but about which we are ignorant), but something that is *logically* possible (even though we may know that it is physically impossible). It is, for instance, a fact that cats have four legs. It is possible that a deformed cat may have five legs. And when I use the word "possible" here, I mean that, although I have never seen a cat with five legs, I do not rule out the possibility that such a cat exists. But I should not say it was possible in the same sense of "possible" that a cat with nine legs exists. Even so, it is conceivable that in another sense of "possible" such a possibility does exist. The statement that there is a cat with nine legs is in this sense a picture of a possible fact as opposed to an actual fact.

Wittgenstein says that whether facts are possible de-

[21] "If I know an object, I also know all its possible occurrences in states of affairs. (Every one of these possibilities must be part of the nature of the object.) A new possibility cannot be discovered later." Ibid. 2.0123 (p.9).
[22] "In order to tell whether a picture is true or false we must compare it with reality." Ibid. 2.223 (p.19). Wittgenstein goes on to say: "It is impossible to tell from the picture alone whether it is true or false." Ibid. 2.224 (p.19). "There are no pictures that are true a priori." Ibid. 2.225 (p.19).

pends on the nature of the objects. To know the nature of an object is to know its internal properties.[23] Internal properties are those which an object must necessarily possess, properties which it is unthinkable that it should *not* possess.[24] Clearly this is not a very precise criterion, for the border line between the thinkable and the unthinkable is obscure and controversial. However, if I ask about the dimensions of the pencil on the table, I cannot be told that it has no dimensions. The property of having dimensions is a necessary one; it is unthinkable that a pencil should be without dimensions and still be a pencil. Thus elementary sentences which say something about the dimensions of the pencil are pictures, although only one of those pictures would be the true picture, namely that one which expressed the correct dimensions of the pencil. Another internal property is motion; the pencil must either be in motion or not in motion. A third is location; the pencil must either be in one place or in another. On the other hand, the pencil itself cannot be a constituent of the facts concerning, for example, intelligence, kindness, or interest in music. The assertion that a pencil is intelligent (or not intelligent) or kind (or not kind) or interested (or not interested) in music—such an assertion is neither a picture nor indeed a statement, it is just nonsense. If objects of a totally different kind from pencils are being considered, their internal properties will also be different. For example, if we speak of pleasure, we can ask about its intensity and duration, but not about its dimensions or color.

Such examples are so simple and obvious that they may seem naive and rather boring. But this question

[23] "If I am to know an object, though I need not know its external properties, I must know all its internal properties." Ibid. 2.01231 (p.9).

[24] "A property is internal if it is unthinkable that its object should not possess it." Ibid. 4.123 (p.53).

of logical form leads to philosophical problems that are not so simple, and which are of considerable interest. Wittgenstein argues, however, that the traditional problems of philosophy are like those questions about the intelligence of a pencil or the color of pleasure.[25] The historically developed language, which Wittgenstein calls "everyday language," is clothed in such a way that its logical form is not immediately apparent; it is veiled, and the business of logico-philosophical analysis is to unveil it.[26] Wittgenstein sees the outstanding example of such logico-philosophical analysis in Russell's analysis of such propositions as "The round square does not exist."[27]

[25] "Most of the propositions and questions to be found in philosophical works are not false but nonsensical. Consequently we cannot give any answer to questions of this kind, but can only establish that they are nonsensical. Most of the propositions and questions of philosophers arise from our failure to understand the logic of our language. (They belong to the same class as the question whether the good is more or less identical with the beautiful.) And it is not surprising that the deepest problems are in fact *not* problems at all." Ibid. 4.003 (p.37).

[26] "Man possesses the ability to construct languages capable of expressing every sense, without having any idea how each word has meaning or what its meaning is—just as people speak without knowing how the individual sounds are produced.

"Everyday language is a part of the human organism and is no less complicated than it.

"It is not humanly possible to gather immediately from it what the language of logic is.

"Language disguises thought. So much so, that from the outward form of the clothing it is impossible to infer the form of the thought beneath it, because the outward form of the clothing is not designed to reveal the form of the body, but for entirely different purposes.

"The tacit conventions on which the understanding of everyday language depends are enormously complicated." Ibid. 4.002 (pp.35–37).

[27] "All philosophy is a 'critique of language' (though not in Mauthner's sense). It was Russell who performed the service of showing that the apparent logical form of a proposition need not be its real one." Ibid. 4.0031 (p.37).

5

Another important characteristic of language for Wittgenstein lies in the distinction between what can be said and what can be shown. Sometimes he seems to speak as if this were his central point.[28] Now a proposition asserts that a state of affairs exists. This means that it must have the same logical form as the facts. In other words, every proposition must have a certain logical form, hence a sense, if it is to be a proposition at all. To find out whether it is true or false we must see whether it corresponds to reality; but we cannot do this without understanding its sense. We cannot decide if a statement is true unless we know what it means. This leads Wittgenstein to say that every proposition, insofar as it is a genuine proposition, already has a sense, already means something.[29] Thus a proposition cannot state its own sense, it cannot say anything about its own logical form. Suppose I have a gramophone record of Beethoven's Fifth Symphony. I can in a certain sense say that the grooves on the record are a "picture" of the symphony, but I cannot reasonably say that the grooves depict how the grooves depict the symphony. To ask for the grooves to depict at the same time their own "picture" of the symphony would be nonsensical. And according to Wittgenstein it is just as meaningless to demand that a proposition should state its own logical form.

On this point one can agree with Wittgenstein without misgivings. If this is all that is meant by his claim

[28] Vide Anscombe, op. cit., p.161.
[29] "Every proposition must *already* have a sense: it cannot be given a sense by affirmation. Indeed, its sense is just what is affirmed. And the same applies to negation, etc." *Tractatus* 4.064 (p.47).

that "What *can* be shown *cannot* be said" nobody will dissent.[30] But Wittgenstein is saying more than this. He claims not only that a proposition cannot say anything about its own form, but also that *no proposition whatever* can say anything about the form of *p*. No proposition can say anything about the logical form of any proposition; the logical form can only be *shown*. Hence it is the task of philosophy not to express the logical form of propositions but to analyze them in such a way that their logical form is uncovered, revealed, displayed.[31] Here Wittgenstein is not so easy to follow. It is hard to see why one proposition should not be able to state anything about the logical form of another proposition. When Russell, for example, talks of the logical form of the proposition "The round square does not exist," why should it be said that he is attempting the impossible? Besides, the *Tractatus* itself is a book that deals mainly with the logical form of propositions, and thus a book which does what it says cannot be done. It is hard to disagree with Russell, who in his introduction to the *Tractatus* writes: "What causes hesitation is the fact that Mr. Wittgenstein manages to say a great deal about what cannot be said,

[30] "What *can* be shown *cannot* be said." Ibid. 4.1212 (p.51). And: "Propositions cannot represent logical form: it is mirrored in them. What finds its reflection in language, language cannot represent. What expresses *itself* in language, *we* cannot express by means of language.

"Propositions *show* the logical form of reality. They display it." Ibid. 4.121 (p.51).

[31] "Philosophy aims at the logical clarification of thoughts. Philosophy is not a body of doctrine but an activity. A philosophical work consists essentially of elucidations. Philosophy does not result in 'philosophical propositions' but rather in the clarification of propositions.

"Without philosophy thoughts are, as it were, cloudy and indistinct: its task is to make them clear and give them sharp boundaries." Ibid. 4.112 (p.49).

thus suggesting to a skeptical reader that possibly there may be some loophole through a hierarchy of language or some other exit."[32] Wittgenstein himself admits that his book says what cannot be said, but he thinks the book has a purpose even so, to be used and discarded. It is like a ladder; and one must throw it away after one has climbed up it.[33]

If Wittgenstein persists in the belief that the logical form of language can only be shown, this may be due to his view that its function is not only to depict, but to depict in the same way that curves and maps depict what they represent as curves and maps.[34] A fever chart, for example, shows the temperature curve of the patient. But neither this nor any curve can be a curve showing the method that is used to depict the fever. This can, of course, be explained orally or in writing, but it cannot be shown on any curve. Nor can a map itself show how the various signs represent various features of the landscape. Of course, the legend may tell us that a cross designates a church, a green patch wooded country, and a brown patch hilly terrain, and so forth, but one could not maintain that these instructions about the meanings of the signs could be given by the signs themselves.[35]

[32] Ibid. p.xxi.
[33] "My propositions serve as elucidations in the following way: anyone who understands me eventually recognizes them as nonsensical, when he has used them—as steps—to climb up beyond them. (He must, so to speak, throw away the ladder after he has climbed up it.)

"He must transcend these propositions and then he will see the world aright." Ibid. 6.54 (p.151).
[34] Vide Gilbert Ryle, "Ludwig Wittgenstein," in *Analysis*, XII, 1, p.5.
[35] At one point Wittgenstein expresses this matter thus: "No proposition can make a statement about itself, because a propositional sign cannot be contained in itself (that is the whole 'theory of types')." *Tractatus* 3.332 (p.31). The "theory of types"

Perhaps one could modify a little Wittgenstein's paradoxical remarks about his own theories. For what does it mean to claim that something cannot be *said?* It does not mean it cannot be uttered, nor does it mean—and this is the crucial point—that it cannot be understood. Indeed, Wittgenstein says explicitly that those who have understood him will see that his propositions are nonsensical. To be nonsensical is not to be incomprehensible. The point is that what is nonsensical is neither true nor false. In other words, it is not a picture; it depicts nothing, and therefore says nothing. Wittgenstein's propositions are like the oral or written instructions which explain how a map depicts a landscape or a chart depicts a fever. Clearly, if one maintains that to say something is to depict something, instructions of this kind, however useful or necessary, *say* nothing. And since Wittgenstein does insist in this way that saying is depicting, it follows that, in his view, explanations of how the pictures depict the facts do not themselves say anything.

6

Another problem arises here. Wittgenstein, we have seen, believes that while the so-called logical unit of language is the elementary proposition which depicts a state of affairs, most of the propositions that are uttered in language are not elementary propositions, but combinations of elementary propositions. They are combinations in the sense that their truth-value—that

is Russell's. Briefly, it states that a class and members of a class belong to different logical types and thus possess different logical categories. In this connection it becomes apparent that Russell's famous paradox "Is the class of classes not members of themselves itself a member of itself?" is based on a question that is illegitimate.

is, whether they are true or false—depends entirely on the truth-value of the elementary propositions of which they are made up. At the same time, Wittgenstein denies that any proposition can be more—or less—than those elementary propositions of which it is composed. For this reason, he calls such propositions "truth-functions," that is, propositions whose truth-value depends on, or is a function of, the truth-values of elementary propositions.

No doubt there are truth-functions. Take the proposition: "The room is empty and the window is open." The proposition is a truth-function because its truth-value is a function of the truth-values of the two propositions "The room is empty" and "The window is open."[36] Again, let us consider the proposition "Possibly Brown *and* Smith are present, but at least one of them is here." This proposition is also a truth-function, for its truth-value depends on the truth-value of two propositions, "Brown is present" and "Smith is present." If either one of these propositions is true, then the truth-function is true. Or, more precisely, the truth-function is false only if both these propositions are false.

The point may seem a trivial one. But the difficulties that arise in the analysis of so-called truth-functions reveal its importance. Let us begin with the proposition "All the inhabitants of this house receive a pension." If there are three inhabitants, this proposition is a truth-function of the three propositions "Smith

[36] It might be argued that the two propositions "The room is empty" and "The window is open" are not elementary propositions. But if these two propositions are not elementary propositions, then they are themselves truth-functions composed of elementary propositions, and their truth-value will determine the truth-value of the propositions "The room is empty" and "The window is open" and also of the truth-function "The room is empty and the window is open."

receives a pension," "Brown receives a pension," and "Robinson receives a pension." Now, suppose that instead of speaking of a definitely limited class like that of the inhabitants of the house, I speak of an unlimited class. Suppose I speak of the class of all snow. I may say "All snow melts at o° centigrade," or, rather less elaborately, "Snow melts at o° centigrade." Of which proposition is this proposition a truth-function? I could of course invent the proposition "This snow melts at o° C." But such propositions would only be considered as mere *samples*. No matter how many propositions of the form "This snow melts at o° C." one had, their sum total would by no means cover "all snow," for this proposition refers not only to all snow that has hitherto been observed, but to all snow whenever or wherever it may be observed. Hence it is highly questionable whether the proposition "All snow melts at o° C." is a truth-function.[37]

A further problem is raised by hypothetical propositions, that is, those of the form "if such and such, then so and so." Suppose I say, "If this is snow, then it will melt at o° C." To call this a truth-function is to indicate that its truth-value will depend on the truth-value of the propositions "This is snow" and "It will melt at o° C." The dependency, or the functional relationship, will be such that the proposition "If this is snow, then it will melt at o° C." will be true in all cases except the one where the proposition "This is snow" is

[37] There is a tendency to express such propositions in the form "If something is snow, then it will melt at o° C." In other words, it is not a proposition used to make a statement about something actually in existence. In this form, the proposition does not say that there is any snow, but only that *if* something is snow, then it will melt at o° C. The proposition is used as an inference-license. It licenses us to pass from the fact, if and when it is ascertained, that there is snow, to the fact that it will melt at o° C.

true and the proposition "It will melt at o° C." is false. However, if this is all it comes to, a mere matter of general propositions—"If *p* then *q*" (where *p* and *q* represent any assertion whatever)—being true, except in those cases where *p* is true and *q* false, then it is hard to see why propositions like "If it is Thursday today then Denmark is a kingdom" should not also be true. Thus it seems that more than the mere truth-values of *p* and *q* must determine the truth-value of "If *p* then *q*." And all this shows that there are difficulties in maintaining the view that all nonelementary propositions are truth-functions of elementary propositions.

7

Wittgenstein claims, as we have seen, that there can be no advance knowledge of whether a certain elementary proposition is true or false. This must be determined in each case by comparing the proposition with reality.[38] In other words, all truth-functions are composed of elementary propositions and the truth of these is empirically determined. This suggests that the truth-value of all truth-functions must be ascertained empirically. So we seem to have come to the following conclusions:

(1) The truth-value of a truth-function depends entirely on the truth-value of its elementary propositions.

(2) The truth-value of the elementary proposition is determined empirically.

[38] For example, he writes: "In order to tell whether a picture is true or false we must compare it with reality." *Tractatus* 2.223 (p.19).

And from these two premises we reach this conclusion:

(3) The truth-value of a truth-function is determined empirically.

Now it is easy to see that this conclusion (3) is not always the case. Consider the truth-function "Either it is raining or it is not raining." Obviously this proposition is always true regardless of the truth-value of the elementary proposition. The proposition "Either it is raining or it is not raining" is true no matter what the state of the weather may be. Wittgenstein calls such truth-functions that cannot possess the truth-value "false" tautologies. The truth-value of a tautology is not determined empirically because it does not deal with anything empirical; it does not deal with reality at all. Nevertheless, a tautology is true; it is a necessary truth, true by logical necessity. A tautology bears a clear relation to a contradiction—it would always be false to say it is both raining and not raining; and such a statement would not be a proposition about the weather at all.

What Wittgenstein is saying is that propositions about reality, his "pictures of facts" are not necessarily true or false; while propositions which *are* necessarily true or false are not statements about reality. If anybody really doubted the truth of the proposition "Either it is raining or it is not raining," we should try to convince him, not by showing him the weather, but by explaining to him the meaning of the logical constants "either," "or" and "not."

According to Wittgenstein, all propositions in logic are tautologies. They are in a sense degenerate propositions. A logically necessary proposition can be obtained only when the conditions of agreement with reality cancel one another.[39]

When one proposition is held to be a logical consequence of another, this too, for Wittgenstein, is a form of tautology. From the two truth-functions "Either it is raining or the sun is shining" and "It is not raining" we can derive the proposition "The sun is shining." To call this a tautology is to say that nothing new has been added to the truth-functions "Either it is raining or the sun is shining" and "It is not raining" by adding the conclusion "The sun is shining." In other words, the following truth-functions are true (or false) under exactly the same conditions:

(1) "Either it is raining or the sun is shining. But it is not raining."

(2) "Either it is raining or the sun is shining. But it is not raining and the sun is shining."

One proposition deduced from another proposition does not say any more about reality than the proposition from which it is deduced. To deduce in this way is not to investigate or discover any features of reality; it is to work on propositions by virtue of the meanings ascribed to the logical constants. In order to observe a logical consequence, it is necessary to understand the meanings of the individual logical constants. Logical necessity or logical impossibility are not determined

[39] "Tautologies and contradictions are not pictures of reality. They do not represent any possible situations. For the former admit *all* possible situations and the latter *none.*

"In a tautology, the conditions of agreement with the world—the representational relations—cancel one another, so that it does not stand in any representational relation to reality." Ibid. 4.462 (p.69).

by the world, by what is "depicted," but by what "depicts," namely, the propositions.[40]

Yet, in a way, logic does tell us something about the world. A proposition and the fact it depicts have the same logical structure. The proposition is able to depict the fact because it shares its logical structure. On the other hand, there is no logical necessity about the logical structures that states of affairs have. Their logical structures can be observed, but not figured out by rational demonstration. Thus it can be said that language by its logical form reveals the logical structure of reality. Deciding which propositions are tautologies— that is, propositions where the conditions for being in agreement with reality cancel one another so that they picture nothing—depends on the logical properties of language and thus of the world.[41] Wittgenstein thus argues that tautologies, and therefore logic, do disclose something about reality.[42]

[40] "There is no compulsion making one thing happen because another has happened. The only necessity that exists is *logical* necessity." Ibid. 6.37 (p.143). Or again, "Just as the only necessity that exists is *logical* necessity, so too the only impossibility that exists is *logical* impossibility." Ibid. 6.375 (p.145).

[41] "The fact that the propositions of logic are tautologies *shows* the formal—logical—properties of language and the world.

"The fact that a tautology is yielded by *this particular way* of connecting its constituents characterizes the logic of its constituents.

"If propositions are to yield a tautology when they are connected in a certain way, they must have certain structural properties. So their yielding a tautology when combined *in this way* shows that they possess these structural properties." Ibid. 6.12 (pp.121–23).

[42] "The propositions of logic describe the scaffolding of the world, or rather they represent it. They have no 'subject matter.' They presuppose that names have meaning and elementary propositions sense, and that is their connection with the world. It is clear that something about the world must be indicated by the fact that certain combinations of symbols—whose essence

8

Language is characterized by its logical form; and insofar as propositions depict reality, the logical form of language is governed by that of reality. Nothing can be said without expressing this form. Indeed, language is capable only of talking about—describing, expressing, characterizing—what is real, what is factually and logically possible. What lies outside the realm of the logically possible cannot be described. Not only can it not be described, it cannot be thought. For a logical picture of a fact is a thought.[43]

---

involves the possession of a determinate character—are tautologies. This contains the decisive point. We have said that some things are arbitrary in the symbols that we use and that some things are not. In logic it is only the latter that express: but this means that logic is not a field in which *we* express what we will with the help of signs, but rather one in which the nature of the natural and inevitable signs speaks for itself. If we know the logical syntax of any sign language, then we have already been given all the propositions of logic." Ibid. 6.124 (p.129).

[43] "A logical picture of facts is a thought.

" 'A state of affairs is thinkable'—this means that we can picture it to ourselves.

"The totality of true thought is a picture of the world.

"A thought contains the possibility of the situation of which it is the thought. What is thinkable is possible, too.

"Thought can never be anything illogical, since, if it were, we should have to think illogically." Ibid. 3, 3.001, 3.01, 3.02, 3.03 (p.19).

It is worth mentioning Ramsey's criticism of this point: he calls it typically scholastic. He says it is like saying the rules of a game such as bridge cannot be broken, on the grounds that if one breaks them, one is no longer playing bridge. See F. P. Ramsey, *The Foundations of Mathematics* (p.269). I am not convinced by Ramsey's argument. If someone asks why the rules of bridge can't be broken, we might answer, of course a man can break them, but if he does, he will not be playing bridge. And to someone who asks why language can't be used illogically, we

36

By a logical picture of a fact Wittgenstein means the proposition that has the same logical form as the fact. For clearly a fact as such cannot be a thought. It is a fact that there is a book on the table, but its being there doesn't depend on whether someone thinks it is there. But can a proposition ever be a thought? If by proposition I mean the series of little black marks on the paper or the series of sounds I produce with the voice, then it would be absurd to maintain that a proposition is the same as the thought. But "proposition" can also mean what is said by the utterance; in which case, it does not depend on whether it is written or spoken. The proposition remains unchanged if, instead of saying that the book is on the table, I write it down or express it in deaf-and-dumb language. The proposition is not dependent on its being formulated in a more or less elegant or stylish way; this does not matter, so long as it is unambiguous. The proposition can be more or less concealed by the grammatical form of the sentence. And a proposition will be most clearly expressed in a sentence which can be completely analyzed, that is, a sentence so worded that its logical form is fully shown. So, in one sense, a proposition is something linguistic; in another sense, something nonlinguistic. It is nonlinguistic in the sense that it does not depend on whether it is in French, Danish, or Swedish; written in pen or pencil; spoken in a loud or soft voice. But it is linguistic in the sense that it demands articulation. It makes no more sense to speak of a proposition that has never been expressed, than to speak of a thought that has never been thought.

Just as the concept "thought" is logically dependent on men who can think, so the concept "proposition"

---

might say, of course he can do it if he wants to, but if he does, he won't be able to *say* anything—to depict actual or possible facts.

is logically dependent on men who can use language. Thus the identification of a proposition with a thought is not absurd. But the concept "thought" must itself be understood correctly. For "thought" may mean a complex of psychological factors, a phenomenon of consciousness. It may be an image, or a representation, or perhaps just a talking to oneself, but whatever it is, one cannot reasonably hold that a thought, in this sense of "thought," is a proposition. But if a thought is not understood psychologically, but taken rather as that which the thought comprises, or, better still, proposes, then it becomes almost a truism to say that a proposition is a thought. In other words, Wittgenstein's argument that a logical picture of a fact is a thought is unexceptionable, provided it is agreed that "a logical picture of a fact" is a proposition. This means that everything that can be thought can be given linguistic expression. And the classical problem of finding the conditions and limits of thought, and so of knowledge, now turns into the problem of determining the conditions and limits of what can be said—and of what *cannot* be said. Thus the investigation of the logical structure of thought and knowledge becomes an investigation of the logical structure of language.

Wittgenstein claims that the limits of language and of the world coincide. The logical limits of language are the limits both of what can be said and what can be thought, and therefore of all that can be said to exist.

A claim that something does not exist must rest on a factual investigation. One can deny the existence only of something which could conceivably exist. For it would be impossible to base the denial of the existence of something on the topic of language alone. To do this would be to commit the error against which Wittgenstein repeatedly warns us: trying to say that which cannot be said.[44]

It is only about facts that anything can be said. One can say what is the case in one situation or another. One can depict facts. But one can say nothing about the universe as a whole, for the universe is the totality of facts, and it cannot without paradox (cf. Russell's theory of types) be maintained that the totality of facts is itself a fact. Besides, it would be to set a limit to the thinkable, and a boundary beyond which the unthinkable lies cannot be drawn.[45]

To say that no proposition can be about the universe as a whole is the same as saying that no thought can be about the universe as a whole, and to wish to think such a thought is to wish to think what cannot be thought and to know what cannot be known. Thus Wittgenstein concludes that the metaphysician's aspiration to know the universe as a whole is doomed to disappointment.

9

It is here that Wittgenstein introduces the concept of the mystical. He does not define it or explain it, but apparently he means by the mystical that which it

[44] *"The limits of my language* mean the limits of my world.

"Logic pervades the world: the limits of the world are also its limits.

"So we cannot say in logic, 'The world has this in it, and this, but not that.'

"For that would appear to presuppose that we were excluding certain possibilities, and this cannot be the case, since it would require that logic should go beyond the limits of the world; for only in that way could it view those limits from the other side as well." *Tractatus* 5.6, 5.61 (p.115).

[45] See Wittgenstein's remarks on this subject in the preface to the *Tractatus*.

would be nonsensical to discuss, describe or even to think, because language cannot logically be employed about it. On the other hand, the mystical is associated with *feeling*—something which can be revealed but not put into words.[46] In this sense, Wittgenstein might be called a mystic. And he is a mystic precisely because he rejects metaphysics. If metaphysics means a philosophy of the universe as a whole, or a philosophy about the transcendental (that which cannot be established in the same way as ordinary facts, but has to be demonstrated by pure reason), then, of course, according to Wittgenstein, metaphysics is impossible.[47] So the mystical is not an insight which language is powerless to express, nor is it an assertion or conjecture about language.

I shall end this short exposition of the *Tractatus* by quoting some passages which indicate the sort of problem Wittgenstein considers to be beyond the limits of science (or of thought or language) and so belonging to the mystical—that which must be "consigned to silence":

> "The sense of the world must lie outside the world. In the world everything is as it is, and every-

[46] "To view the world *sub specie aeterni* is to view it as a whole —a limited whole.

"Feeling the world as a limited whole." *Tractatus* 6.45 (p. 149).

[47] In accordance with this Wittgenstein says: "The correct method in philosophy would really be the following: to say nothing except what can be said, i.e. the propositions of natural science—i.e. something that has nothing to do with philosophy—and then, whenever someone else wanted to say something metaphysical, to demonstrate to him that he had failed to give a meaning to certain signs in his propositions. Although it would not be satisfying to the other person—he would not have the feeling that we were teaching him philosophy—*this* method would be the only strictly correct one." Ibid. 6.53 (p.151).

thing happens as it does happen: *in* it no value exists—and if it did, it would have no value.

"If there is any value that does have value, it must lie outside the whole sphere of what happens and is the case. For all that happens and is the case is accidental.

"What makes it nonaccidental cannot lie *within* the world, since if it did it would itself be accidental.

"It must lie outside the world.[48]

"And so it is impossible for them to be propositions of ethics.

"Propositions can express nothing of what is higher.[49]

"It is clear that ethics cannot be put into words.[50]

"Death is not an event in life: we do not live to experience death.

"If we take eternity to mean not infinite temporal duration but timelessness, the eternal life belongs to those who live in the present.

"Our life has no end in just the way in which our visual field has no limits.[51]

"Not only is there no guarantee of the temporal immortality of the human soul, that is to say of its eternal survival after death; but in any case this assumption completely fails to accomplish the purpose for which it has always been intended. Or is some riddle solved by my surviving forever? Is not this eternal life as much a riddle as my present life? The solution of the riddle of life and space and time lies *outside* space and time.

[48] Ibid. 6.41 (p.145).
[49] Ibid. 6.42 (p.145).
[50] Ibid. 6.421 (p.147).
[51] Ibid. 6.4311 (p.147).

"(It is not the solution of any problem of natural science that is required.)[52]

"*How* things are in the world is a matter of complete indifference for what is higher. God does not reveal himself *in* the world.[53]

"It is not *how* things are in the world that is mystical, but *that* it exists.[54]

"We feel that even when *all possible* scientific questions have been answered, the problems of life remain completely untouched. Of course there are then no questions left, and this itself is their answer.[55]

"The solution of the problem of life is seen in the vanishing of the problem.

"(Is not this the reason why those who have found after a long period of doubt that the sense of life became clear to them have then been unable to say what constituted that sense?)"[56]

[52] Ibid. 6.4312 (pp.147–49).
[53] Ibid. 6.432 (p.149).
[54] Ibid. 6.44 (p.145).
[55] Ibid. 6.52 (p.149).
[56] Ibid. 6.521 (pp.149–51).

III

The *Tractatus* and Logical Positivism

1

The *Tractatus* is a book of just over eighty pages, but it has exercised a greater influence on twentieth-century philosophy than almost any other single work. The dominant philosophical school in the years between the wars was that of logical positivism. And although logical positivism derived something or other from a variety of sources, its decisive impulse and central inspiration came from the *Tractatus*. Logical positivism was formulated in Vienna in the 1920's by a group of philosophers generally known as the *Wiener Kreis* or "Vienna Circle." One of the works they studied together was the *Tractatus*. The author was living in or near Vienna at this time, but he never attended the discussions or adhered to the *Kreis*. This aloofness, strange as it may seem, was very characteristic of Wittgenstein. But through Moritz Schlick, the real leader of the *Wiener Kreis*, Wittgenstein had some contact with it, and some indirect share in its deliberations. However, it would be a great mistake to assume on the strength of this, as some have done, that Wittgenstein was a logical positivist. One can see that he was not if only one understands what logical positivists believe. For although some of the ideas in the *Tractatus* have become fundamental tenets of logical positivism, there are basic disagreements between that doctrine and what is said in the *Tractatus*.

Now one of the central points of logical positivism is that the task of philosophy, far from solving the traditional philosophical problems or determining the truth of philosophical propositions, is simply to clarify the meaning of such problems and propositions. Thus, philosophy does not lead to a collection of philosophical propositions, but it does lead to a better understanding of the meanings of various propositions, and —last but not least—to a realization that certain metaphysical propositions are meaningless.[1] As to how the

[1] In a lecture entitled "The Future of Philosophy," Moritz Schlick wrote: "In fact, before I go any farther, let me state shortly and clearly that I believe science should be defined as 'the pursuit of truth' and philosophy as 'the pursuit of meaning.' Socrates has set the example of the true philosophic method for all time." (First printed in *Publications on Philosophy*, the College of the Pacific, U.S.A., 1932. Reprinted in *Basic Problems of Philosophy*, ed. by Bronstein, Krikorian and Wiener, N.Y., 1947. The quotation is taken from this work, p.739). Schlick also says: "Our conclusion is that philosophy was misunderstood when it was thought that philosophical results could be expressed in propositions, and that there could be a system of philosophy consisting of a system of propositions which could represent the answers

meaning of a proposition is to be ascertained, the answer is to invoke the famous verification principle—one of the key tenets of logical positivism. According to this principle, one understands the meaning of a proposition if one knows what is required for it to be true; in other words, if one knows how it could be verified. Any child knows the meaning of the proposition "It is raining" because any child is capable of deciding when it is true and when it is not true—any child can verify it. Logical positivism claims that if the conditions for the verification of a proposition are not known, then its meaning cannot be known.

Of course it is of small importance if I, or any other person, happen not to know the conditions for the verification of a certain proposition and therefore not to know its meaning. But it is a matter of considerable importance and interest if it is found that a particular proposition has no conditions for verification at all, for this is not a case of someone being ignorant, a case that can be remedied by suitable instruction; in this case, the proposition has no meaning at all. It is not due to some shortcoming in me or anybody else that no meaning can be found; there is none to find, nothing to be known except that there is nothing to be known; the proposition is meaningless. Indeed, it cannot properly be called a proposition at all, for a proposition is either true or false, and a proposition that has no conditions for verification can be neither true nor false. Such sentences, which appear from their grammatical form to be propositions, which they are not, are called pseudopropositions by logical positivists.

---

to 'philosophical' questions. There are no specific philosophical truths which would contain the solutions of specific 'philosophical' problems, but philosophy has the task of finding the meanings of all problems and their solutions. It must be defined as the activity of finding meaning." (Ibid., p.743.)

Empirical propositions are the only ones that logical positivism regards as genuine, for they are the only kind that can be verified. Logical positivism admits, of course, the propositions of mathematics and logic although these are empirically empty. Wittgenstein was supposed to have proved that these particular propositions were tautologies, saying nothing about the real world. Logical and mathematical propositions are not *verified*, they are *demonstrated*. They are not true in the sense that empirical propositions can be true—they are *valid*. On the other hand, philosophical or metaphysical propositions are neither empirical nor tautological—they can be neither verified nor demonstrated; they are neither true nor valid—they are simply meaningless. They are not empirical, for if they were, their truth-value could be ascertained by observation; and this cannot be done in the case of metaphysical propositions. A proposition which could be verified empirically would not belong to metaphysics but to the natural sciences. And as metaphysical propositions have no truth-conditions, they have no meaning either. If, on the other hand, they were tautologies, there could be no dispute about their validity, as there actually is among philosophers.

2

It is not difficult to detect a connection between the *Tractatus* and these central tenets of logical positivism. The view that philosophy cannot yield a series of propositions but that it is an activity, the view that logical and mathematical propositions are tautologies and thus empirically empty and that empirical propositions cannot be true by logical necessity, and the view that the meaning of a proposition is identical with its truth-conditions—all these views are to be found in the

Tractatus. And yet, at least in regard to the last of these views, Wittgenstein's position is not altogether clear. At one point in the *Tractatus*, he says that to understand a proposition means to know what is the case if it is true.[2] And this looks like a plain statement of the principle that the meaning of a proposition is identical with its truth-conditions; therefore it also seems to say—at least to imply—that a proposition without truth-conditions is without meaning. But, in fact, Wittgenstein refused to accept the universal application of this principle by logical positivism. He wanted it to be taken not as a firm principle but rather as a "rule of thumb,"[3] as he called it, not as a theoretical generalization but as a piece of advice which might commonly be followed to advantage.[4] It must be ad-

[2] "To understand a proposition means to know what is the case if it is true. (One can understand it, therefore, without knowing whether it is true.) It is understood by anyone who understands its constituents." *Tractatus* 4.024 (p.41). See also 4.063 (pp. 45–7).

[3] See, for instance, G. E. Moore's "Wittgenstein's Lectures in 1930–33," in *Mind* (LXIII, 249, p.14): "Near the beginning of (I) he made the famous statement 'The sense of a proposition is the way in which it is verified,' but in (II) he said this only meant 'You can determine the meaning of a proposition by asking how it is verified,' and went on to say 'This is necessarily a mere rule of thumb because "verification" means different things and because in some cases, the question "How is it verified?" makes no sense.' "

[4] Wittgenstein is supposed once to have made the following statement: "I used at one time to say that, in order to get clear how a certain sentence is used, it was a good idea to ask oneself the question 'How could one verify such an assertion?' But this is just one way among others of getting clear about the use of a word or a sentence. For example, another question which is often very useful to ask oneself is 'How is this word learned? How would people set about teaching a child this word?' But some people have turned this suggestion about asking for the verification into a dogma—as if I'd been advancing a *theory* about meaning." (From "Ludwig Wittgenstein," by D.A.T.G. and A.C.J., *The Australasian Journal of Philosophy*, XXIX, 2, p.79.)

mitted, however, that these reservations concerning the verification principle are not to be found in the *Tractatus*; and therefore those who claim that it was Wittgenstein who first put forward the verification principle have done so not only in good faith, but also with good reasons.[5] And again, even if the verification principle is not explicitly formulated in the *Tractatus*, there may still be a case for saying that it is implicitly upheld in that treatise.

For if every nontautological proposition is either an elementary proposition or a truth-function of elementary propositions, and if the truth-value is (as Wittgenstein says) not the consequence of anything or derived from logical necessity, then it follows that the truth-value of every nontautological proposition must be (as Wittgenstein says, again) determined by comparing it with reality.[6] Thus a proposition which cannot be compared with reality is neither an elementary proposition nor a truth-function of elementary propositions, so it must either be a tautology or a meaningless expression.

On the other hand, it must be admitted that Wittgenstein's remark about the truth-value of an elementary proposition being determined by comparing it with reality is a remark that can be—and has been—interpreted in different ways. For example, there has

[5] See, for example, Rudolf Carnap, "The Old and New Logic," in *Logical Positivism* (ed. by A. J. Ayer), p.146. See also Moritz Schlick, "Meaning and Verification," in *Readings in Philosophical Analysis* (pp.147 ff.) However, G. J. Warnock argues that Schlick misrepresents Wittgenstein's views in this article. See Warnock's "Verification and the Use of Language," in *Revue Internationale de Philosophie*, 17–18, 1951, facs. 3–4, pp.307 ff. The difference between the *Tractatus* and Schlick's views is also stressed by G. E. M. Anscombe in *An Introduction to Wittgenstein's Tractatus* (pp.152 ff.).
[6] *Tractatus* 2.223 (p.19).

been some controversy[7] as to whether the truth-value should be understood to rest on sensory observation and ostensive definitions. But perhaps it is not so very important what Wittgenstein himself had in mind. It is more important to admit that in spite of Wittgenstein's failure to indicate more explicitly what is entailed by the comparison of elementary propositions with reality, the logical positivists were justified in concluding that it must be sensory observations which determine whether a proposition is true or false. If no conceivable sensory observations are relevant to the truth-value of a proposition, then it is clearly impossible to decide the truth-value by a comparison between the proposition and reality. In this case, it can be neither an elementary proposition nor a truth-function of a proposition, and as on Wittgenstein's analysis every proposition must be either one or the other, it cannot therefore be a genuine proposition and must be meaningless.

One thing, however, is certain—Wittgenstein's idea of the verification principle and its use differed from that of the logical positivists. It is arguable whether the logical positivists are right in drawing from the *Tractatus* conclusions which Wittgenstein was unable or unwilling to draw, or whether the logical positivists have misunderstood the *Tractatus* and drawn conclusions that cannot be justified. It is almost impossible to settle this matter because of the aphoristic style[8] of the *Tractatus*; though perhaps one could say that nothing in the actual text *contradicts* the logical positivists' in-

[7] See, among others, the works by Schlick, Warnock and Anscombe mentioned in footnote 5, above.
[8] Russell once made this rather sarcastic observation: "Wittgenstein announces aphorisms and leaves the reader to estimate their profundity as best he may." *My Philosophical Development* (p.126).

51

terpretation, no matter what Wittgenstein may have intended to say. In any case, whether the logical positivists have been right or wrong in their reading of the *Tractatus*, this has no bearing on whether they are correct in their view of what constitutes the meaning of a proposition. Even if they are wrong in thinking that their principle of verification was first proposed by Wittgenstein, they may still be right in thinking that this principle is the only acceptable one.

3

On another subject the difference between Wittgenstein and the logical positivists is more pronounced. This is the matter of the mystical. The propositions of language (Wittgenstein says) are either elementary propositions or truth-functions of elementary propositions. An elementary proposition is a picture of a state of affairs. Language is an instrument by which facts are depicted. And as the world is the totality of facts, language depicts what is in the world. Language sets the logical limit of my world.[9] What we cannot speak about we must consign to silence; but Wittgenstein still holds that what we cannot speak about exists.[10] This is not what is spoken in language, it is what is felt—it is the mystical. And it is on this point that the logical positivists are sharply at variance with Wittgenstein. For them, what cannot be said, and therefore cannot be thought, is not an expression of the limits of language. The reason for being silent is that there is nothing to speak about.[11] The antimetaphysi-

[9] *Tractatus* 5.6 (p.115).
[10] Ibid. 6.522 (p.151).
[11] One of the founders of logical positivism, Otto Neurath, writes: "The conclusion of the *Tractatus*, 'whereof one cannot speak, thereof one must be silent,' is at least grammatically mis-

cal attitude of the logical positivists thus differs from that of Wittgenstein. Wittgenstein believed metaphysics to be impossible because it is impossible to formulate metaphysical propositions, *not* because such propositions would be about something that does not exist, but because language cannot make metaphysical assertions.

However, Wittgenstein's position is jeopardized by a certain inconsistency. The reader will recall that in the previous chapter I proposed to modify Wittgenstein's paradoxical statements in the *Tractatus* about propositions that cannot be expressed, by suggesting that what cannot be expressed can nevertheless be understood.[12] But this interpretation is made difficult by the statements in the *Tractatus* in which Wittgenstein seems to identify a proposition with a thought.[13] Such an identification leads to the conclusion that what cannot be said, what cannot be a meaningful statement, cannot be a thought either. And when Wittgenstein says in this way that something is unthinkable, he is not talking psychology. He is not saying it is psychologically impossible to think what cannot be a meaningful proposition; he is saying it is logically impossible.

Now, one could reasonably hold that something which it is psychologically impossible to think never-

leading. It sounds as if there were a 'something' of which we could not speak. We should rather say, 'If one really wishes to avoid the metaphysical attitude entirely, then one will "be silent," but not "about something".' " Quoted from "Sociology and Physicalism," in *Logical Positivism* (ed. A. J. Ayer), p.284.

[12] "My propositions serve as elucidations in the following way: anyone who understands me eventually recognizes them as nonsensical, when he has used them—as steps—to climb up beyond them." *Tractatus* 6.54 (p.151).

[13] "A logical picture of facts is a thought." Ibid. 3 (p.19). And again, "A thought is a proposition with a sense." Ibid. 4 (p.35).

theless exists. But what sense does it make to say that something which it is logically impossible to think nevertheless exists? Well, the answer seems to be that it makes no sense. But to say that X is logically impossible to think is to say that one does not know what X is; what is known can also be logically expressed. And thus to say that one knows what X is and that it is logically impossible to think it is to make two contradictory statements—it would be like saying that one had read about a game that was logically impossible to play, for no matter what one did it would never be in accordance with the rules. To have a game so complicated that it would be psychologically impossible for anyone to learn the rules might be said to be rather futile, but it would be possible for such a game to exist. But if in a game the rules are such that it is logically impossible to obey them, then one could not claim that such a game exists. From this it follows that Wittgenstein could not easily uphold his thesis that the inexpressible exists; and it follows also that the logical positivists have a good case for regarding such a thesis as absurd.

4

We have noticed more than once that Wittgenstein calls language a picture of facts. Language, he says, depicts the logical structure of facts. As each separate fact has only one logical form, it follows that each fact can be correctly depicted by only one proposition, and hence that there is only one language. A language that does not depict facts is not a language. And (as we have seen) language cannot depict its own picturing of facts—its logical form can be shown but not stated. I have already quoted Russell's claim that it should be possible to speak of the logical form of a language, if not in that same language, then in another. The fact that we (including Wittgenstein) do speak of the logical form of language points to the existence of a language in which such statements can be made. We should have to speak of this second language by means of a third language, and so forth. Hence we are led to the idea of a hierarchy of languages. And this argument of Russell's was accepted by, among others, the logical positivists,[14] who thus came to speak not of language but of languages.

Rudolf Carnap, for example, spoke not only of a hierarchy of languages, but also of several languages on a more or less equal footing. He expressed this by means of his celebrated tolerance-principle. In this view, in order to be considered a language, no conditions are demanded. There are no restrictions—the only requirement is that certain rules are established, and these rules then constitute the language in question.[15] Everyone is free to construct his own language, and consequently his own logic.[16]

[14] It is worth noticing that in spite of following Russell's distinction between an *object language* (the language talked about) and a *metalanguage* (in which the language is talked about), Rudolf Carnap was able in his *Logical Syntax of Language* (one of the key works of logical positivism) to formulate the rules of a constructed mathematical language by means of that language itself. However, semantic rules as opposed to syntactical rules (that is, rules about what things are designated by the words as opposed to rules about the connection of words with each other) must be formulated in a metalanguage. See Wittgenstein's remark: "No proposition can make a statement about itself, because a propositional sign cannot be contained in itself (that is the whole 'theory of types')." *Tractatus* 3.332 (p.31).

[15] "It is not our business to set up prohibitions, but to arrive at conventions." Carnap, *Logical Syntax of Languages*, p.51.

[16] "*In logic there are no morals.* Everyone is at liberty to build up his own logic, i.e. his own form of language, as he wishes. All that is required of him is that, if he wishes to discuss it, he must

On this matter logical positivism not only deviates from the *Tractatus*, but is in conflict with one of its fundamental assertions, that language is a picture of reality. Which particular language is chosen depends on practical considerations. No one language is in itself more or less correct than any other, but it may be more or less appropriate for a particular purpose. In the case of a scientific language, for example, it is imperative that the propositions that follow the syntactical rules of the language should be verifiable by means of empirical observation, but it is not imperative for its propositions to be pictures of facts or that its propositions should have the same logical form. Logical positivists cease to speak of facts having a logical form. The task of philosophy is no longer to seek the concealed logical form of a language that depicts the logical form of the facts; rather it is to construct whatever language will best suit different purposes for which language is needed. Among members of the *Wiener Kreis* interest centered on the construction of a language in which the languages of the different sciences—physics, biology, psychology, sociology and so on—could be unified. They wanted to construct a common scientific language. There might be a constructed language of this kind if its logical syntactical rules were such that all the propositions of all the sciences could be derived from them.

Yet, despite this departure of logical positivism from the teaching of the *Tractatus*, the fact remains that, without the *Tractatus*, without Wittgenstein's deep insight into the nature of logic and language, logical positivism would have lacked the rational foundations and the rational force which it has undoubtedly possessed. To a large extent the *Tractatus* gave logical

state his method clearly, and give syntactical rules instead of philosophical arguments." Ibid., p.52.

positivism both its material and its tools. Whether Wittgenstein or Carnap is right on the question where they differ is not our present subject; a further analysis would probably show that they are both partly right, partly wrong. Certainly Wittgenstein's thesis about the inexpressible is unconvincing, while Carnap's tolerance-principle must lead to absurdities.[17] As for the verification principle, time has turned against the logical positivists, and to some extent against Wittgenstein—to the extent that he can be said to have upheld or even formulated the verification principle. But it is worth noting that if time has turned against it, this is very largely due to Wittgenstein's own more mature philosophy, which is not only controversial but decidedly at variance with what is said by the author of the *Tractatus*. So we shall now turn to what is often called "the later Wittgenstein."

[17] G. H. von Wright has this to say about the tolerance-principle: "In the tolerance here under discussion I can see nothing but an expression of weakness and resignation or perhaps more correctly lack of interest in the problems of philosophy. That kind of liberalism is misguided." *Logik, Filosofi och Språk*, pp.176–77.

IV

The *Philosophical Investigations*

1

According to the *Tractatus*, language is a picture of reality: language depicts the logical structure of facts. Wittgenstein's repudiation of this view is one characteristic difference between his earlier and later work, between the *Tractatus* and the *Philosophical Investigations*. Naturally there was a period of transition, a period when Wittgenstein was moving away from the ideas in the *Tractatus* before decisively rejecting them, a period when the ideas in the *Philosophical Investigations* were beginning to take shape. This period is said to have fallen within the years 1930 to 1934. The story of how Wittgenstein came to doubt and then reject the picture theory is this. A Cambridge colleague was the Italian economist Piero Sraffa, with whom Wittgenstein often discussed philosophy.[1] One day when Wittgenstein was defending his view that a proposition has the same logical form as the fact it depicts, Sraffa made a gesture used by Neapolitans to express contempt and asked Wittgenstein what the logical form of that was. According to Wittgenstein's own recollection, it was this question which made him realize that his belief that a fact could have a logical form was untenable.[2]

The repudiation of this belief had far-reaching implications for the whole theory expounded in the *Tractatus*—for the picture theory is a basic one, and, without it, none of the central points of the argument could be sustained. No unbroken line leads from the *Tractatus* to the *Philosophical Investigations*; there is no logical sequence between the two books, but rather a logical gap. The thought of the later work is a negation of the thought of the earlier. But of course the *Philosophical Investigations* is much more than a repudiation of the *Tractatus*—it is that only incidentally. What gives the second book its importance is that it contains the mature philosophy of Wittgenstein. The

[1] In the preface to *Philosophical Investigations* (after mentioning Ramsey's influence on the shaping of the ideas in their work) Wittgenstein writes: "Even more than to this—always certain and forcible—criticism, I am indebted to that which a teacher of this university, Mr. P. Sraffa, for many years increasingly practiced on my thoughts. I am indebted to *this* stimulus for the most consequential ideas of this book." *Philosophical Investigations* (Second Edition, Oxford, 1963) p.X^e. (All quotations from *Philosophical Investigations* are taken from this second, corrected, edition.)

[2] See Malcolm's *Ludwig Wittgenstein: A Memoir* (p.69). It should be observed (as mentioned in a footnote) that Malcolm and Von Wright differ in their accounts of this story.

Philosophical Investigations introduces a new chapter in the history of philosophy. It is not just a continuation or development of the thought of others. It is something wholly original.[3]

2

We have spoken of the well-established idea that a word has meaning in being the name of something. A word, in this view, represents or refers to something, and to ask what a word means is to ask what it stands for. The word "apple" is the name of the fruit that grows on the apple tree, and this fruit is what the word "apple" means. In the same way the word "red" is understood to represent the red color which is seen in various places. No great difficulties are raised by saying that "a red apple" refers to and therefore means a red apple. It becomes more difficult if instead of "a red apple" I say "five red apples." For what does the word "five" refer to? This is much harder to answer. I can point to an apple and a red-colored patch, but I cannot point to the number five. According to Wittgenstein, it would be a mistake to ask what the word "five" means if it is taken as a question about what the word "five" names or refers to. Suppose, says Wittgenstein, that I send someone shopping and give him a slip marked "five red apples." To the shopkeeper it has the following meaning—he goes to the box marked "apples" and opens it; he then looks up the word "red" in a color chart and finds a color sample beside it;

[3] "Wittgenstein's later philosophy is, so far as I can see, entirely outside any philosophical tradition and without literary sources of influence. For this very reason it is exceedingly difficult to understand and characterize. The author of the *Tractatus* learned from Frege and Russell. His problems grew out of theirs. The author of the *Philosophical Investigations* has no ancestor in philosophy." Von Wright, op. cit., p.15.

then he recites the cardinal numbers up to the number 5 and for each number he takes from the box an apple of the color which corresponds to the sample. The test of the shopkeeper's understanding what is written on the slip is that he acts as he does. That he understands "five" is shown by his counting from one to five and stopping (after taking an apple for each number) when he has reached "five." If "four" or "six" had been written on the slip and he, still in good faith, had acted as he did, it would prove that he had not understood the meaning of these cardinal numbers. What is decisive is how the word "five" is used. If one asks what the word "five" names, the question is based on a misunderstanding; the appropriate question is to ask how the word "five" is used.[4]

Now it is possible to imagine a primitive language-situation or language-form—what Wittgenstein calls a language-game—where there would be some reason for maintaining that the meaning of a word is the thing to which it refers. It is conceivable that the conversation between a skilled workman and his mate might consist of names only, that is, the names of the tools needed by the workman and handed to him by his mate every time he mentions one of them. Such a language—or a language-game—consists of names only, and in order to master the language one must learn what the individual names refer to.

Wittgenstein suggests that this language-game comes close to what he calls the Augustinian conception of language. Wittgenstein quotes a remark of St. Augustine in his *Confessions* that he had learned to understand the speech of his elders by understanding which objects were signified by the different words.

[4] "But what is the meaning of the word 'five'?—No such thing was in question here, only how the word 'five' is used." *Philosophical Investigations* §1 (p.3ᵉ).

St. Augustine fancied, according to Wittgenstein, that he had discovered what was essential to all languages (or language-games), namely that all words should have a meaning and that the meaning of each was what it stood for. But this, says Wittgenstein, is true of only one special language-game, and is not true of all language-games. To suppose it is is like someone trying to explain the word "game" by saying that it means moving objects in a certain order about a board; and this of course would be true only of board games, and not of the many other kinds of games there are.[5]

But let us examine the Augustinian language-game a little more closely. Augustine conceived of it as a *naming-game*, that is, as a language mastered by learning the names of the different things. The mastery will be complete when one has learned all the names by *ostensive definition*—by pointing to a thing and at the same time speaking its name. Often such a definition is the only possible one; or so it is said. If I have to explain the meaning of the word "red" to someone, how can I do it better than by pointing to a patch of red color and saying "This color is called red"?

Consider the situation between the workman and his mate. Has the mate learned this language-game as soon as he knows the names of the tools? Certainly not. He knows, for instance, that this particular thing is called a hammer. But what does he suppose the workman means when he says, "Hammer." Does it mean that he is repeating the name to himself? Or is he uncertain, and asking the mate to reassure him that this is really a hammer? Or does it mean that he wants the mate to give him the hammer? Or does it have some further and completely different meaning? The mate who knows only what the word "hammer" stands

[5] Ibid. §3 (p.3e).

for has no way of understanding what the workman means when he says, "Hammer." He has not learned the language-game simply by knowing what the words name. In this particular game, "hammer" means more than a particular tool; it means that this particular tool must be handed to the workman. And the same holds true of the language-game described by St. Augustine. Although St. Augustine had learned what the various words named, he had not yet learned how to *use* them. Therefore he had not yet learned to give or understand orders, to make or understand requests, to ask or understand questions, and so on. Just as learning the names of playing cards or of the pieces in a chess set is not learning to play bridge or to play chess, so to know the names in a language is less than learning how to speak it. A language has been learned only when one can play the various language-games that make up the language concerned; that is to say, when one has learned how to use the words for such purposes as asking questions, describing things and events, giving orders, making requests and promises, evaluating, condemning or naming.

The language-games found in a particular language are expressions of a people's form of life. So a language which can do nothing but command—which has this language-game only—expresses a simpler form of life than a language in which it is possible both to give commands and to ask questions. If in a language one cannot make requests, describe, or ask questions, it means that these human activities do not exist there. We would not find the same form of life as we should in cases where the language can be used to do all these things.[6]

I have mentioned among the different kinds of lan-

[6] "It is easy to imagine a language consisting only of orders and reports in battle.—Or a language consisting only of questions and expressions for answering yes and no. And innumerable others.—

guage-games that of naming, that of assigning names to things and memorizing them. It might well be supposed, in the Augustinian fashion, that to give and learn names—the naming language-game—was the logical basis of the other language-games, just as learning to know the cards is a basis for learning to play the various card games. This amounts to saying that one can learn to speak only by giving and memorizing names. And teaching or learning names is done by ostensive definition. But is it logically necessary to begin with such definitions? According to Wittgenstein, the answer must be no, since ostensive definitions already presuppose a certain knowledge of language.

Suppose, for instance, I want to give an ostensive definition of the word "red." Pointing to a red object, I say, "This is red," or, "This color is red," or just, "Red." This definition will be understood by someone who knows what the word "color" means. Otherwise he will be none the wiser. He may believe with equal justification that "It is red" means that the *shape* of the object is what is referred to as red, or that this *kind* of object is called "red"; or perhaps that "red" is the name of this particular object (as "John" is the name of this particular man); or he may think that it means something about the aesthetic qualities of the object. But if he does not know the meaning of any of the words "color," "common name," "proper name," or "aesthetic," and is therefore unfamiliar with any of these concepts, it is logically impossible for him to understand the word "red" in any of the ways mentioned. If, for example, he cannot yet talk at all, but is just beginning to learn, then starting his instruction

And to imagine a language means to imagine a form of life." Ibid. §19 (p.8e). Elsewhere Wittgenstein writes: "Here the term 'language-*game*' is meant to bring into prominence the fact that *speaking* of language is part of an activity, or a form of life." Ibid. §23 (p.11e).

with an ostensive definition of "red" (speaking the word while pointing to the red color) will tell him nothing. This is not because of his limited skill, but because it is a logical impossibility. This is the basis of Wittgenstein's assertion that ostensive definition presupposes a certain knowledge of the language; hence the naming language-game cannot be a basis for other language-games, but, on the contrary, itself presupposes other language-games. One has to know the language in order to be able to name.[7]

What we have so far argued is this: there can be no definite limit to the possibility of constructing language-games. It is only with regard to particular language-games that it can be said that language consists of names. And even in the case of such languages, it is a mistake to think they can be learned through ostensive definitions, which work only with people who al-

[7] "So one might say: the ostensive definition explains the use—the meaning—of the word when the overall role of the word in the language is clear. Thus if I know that someone means to explain a color-word to me, the ostensive definition 'That is called "sepia"' will help me to understand the word.—And you can say this so long as you do not forget that all sorts of problems attach to the words 'to know' or 'to be clear.'

"One has already to know (or to be able to do) something in order to be capable of asking a thing's name." Ibid. §30 (pp. 14e–15e).

"We may say: only someone who already knows how to do something with it can significantly ask a name." Ibid. §31 (p.15e).

And finally: "Someone coming into a strange country will sometimes learn the language of the inhabitants from the ostensive definitions that they give him; and he will often have to *guess* the meanings of those definitions, and he will guess sometimes right, sometimes wrong.

"And now I think we can say: Augustine describes the learning of human language as if a child came into a strange country and did not understand the language of the country; that is, as if he already had a language, only not this one. Or again as if the child could already *think*, only not yet speak. And 'think' would here mean something like 'talk to oneself.'" Ibid. §32 (pp.15e–16e).

ready have some knowledge of the language. The meaning of a word is learned by discovering its use. And if its use has been learned, its meaning has been learned, too.[8] This also implies that what the word names cannot be its meaning, something which is manifestly evident in the case of proper names. The name "Peter" is the name of a person, but this person is not what the name "Peter" means. When Peter dies it is the bearer of the name "Peter" who dies and not the meaning of the name "Peter." Bearers of proper names live and die; meanings can do neither.[9] Proper names are names par excellence, and, in fact, one never asks what proper names mean. We do not ask, "What does 'Peter' mean?" but "Who is 'Peter'?" It would be absurd to say to anyone who did ask what "Peter" means that it meant a person standing by the window. One might, however, answer that "Peter" meant "rock." But there is a difference in this sense of the word "meaning"—the difference between saying that *rouge* means the color at which I am now pointing and saying that "*rouge*" means "red."

3

We have come a long way from the doctrine of the *Tractatus*. In the *Tractatus* a meaningful proposition

[8] "For a *large* class of cases—though not for all—in which we employ the word 'meaning,' it can be defined thus: the meaning of a word is its use in the language." Ibid. §43 (p. 20e).

[9] "Let us first discuss *this* point of the argument: that a word has no meaning if nothing corresponds to it.—It is important to notice that the word 'meaning' is being used illicitly if it is used to signify the thing that 'corresponds' to the word. That is to confound the meaning of a name with the *bearer* of a name. When Mr. N.N. dies, one says that the bearer of the name dies, not that the meaning dies. And it would be nonsensical to say that, for if the name ceased to have meaning, it would make no sense to say 'Mr. N.N. is dead.'" Ibid. §40 (p.20e).

was said to be one made up of the names of objects, and to serve as a picture of a fact; language depicted the world. In the *Philosophical Investigations* language is no longer said to act like this. Picturing or depicting the world is discarded as a meaningless notion; there are many different language-games, some of which serve to describe, to assert, to report. The countless other language-games that do not describe, assert or report are still languages; and the countless other sentences that do not describe, assert or report are still sentences.[10] In the *Tractatus* a word is meaningful if, and only if, it is a name. In the *Philosophical Investigations*, a word is *not* a name; a word can be *used* as a name, but it can be used in numerous other ways as well.[11]

Now if a language is no longer to be understood as a picture of the world, how else is it to be defined? What

[10] "But how many kinds of sentences are there? Say, assertion, question and command?—There are *countless* kinds, countless different kinds of uses of what we call 'symbols,' 'words,' 'sentences.' And this multiplicity is not something fixed, given once for all; but new types of language, new language-games as we may say, come into existence, and others become obsolete and get forgotten. (We can get a *rough picture* of this from the changes in mathematics)." Ibid. §23 (p.11e).

[11] " 'We name things and then we can talk about them: we can refer to them in talk.'—As if what we did next were given with the mere act of naming. As if there were only a thing called 'talking about a thing.' Whereas, in fact, we do the most various things with our sentences. Think of exclamations alone, with their completely different functions.

Water!
Away!
Ow!
Help!
Fine!
No!

Are you still inclined to call these words 'names of objects'?" Ibid. §27 (p.13e).

do the different language-games have in common that
entitles them to be called a language?[12] Wittgenstein's
answer is simple; they have nothing in common. No
one definite element, no one distinctive property must
be possessed by them all in order for each to qualify
for recognition as a language.

This kind of answer runs against a long tradition. It
seems to be good philosophical common sense to insist that if anything is to be named as something or
other, classified in one way or another, then this must
be done in virtue of some property which entitles it to
be so named or classified. Members of the class of all
red things have in common the color "red," and members of the class of triangles have in common the characteristic of being geometric figures of a certain type.
But according to Wittgenstein, the members of the
class of all language-games have no such property in
common. This means that the concept of "language"
cannot be defined. A triangle can be defined as a figure
having three angles and three straight lines, and "red"
can be defined ostensively—"the color that looks like
this." But nothing of this sort can be said about a language—it has no defining property.[13]

Wittgenstein defends this assertion by comparing

[12] "Here we come up against the great question that lies behind
all these considerations.—For someone might object against me:
'You take the easy way out. You talk about all sorts of language-
games, but have nowhere said what the essence of a language-
game, and hence of language, is: what is common to all these
activities, and what makes them into language, or parts of language. So you let yourself off the very part of the investigation
that once gave you yourself most headache, the part about the
general form of propositions and of language.'" Ibid. §65
(p.31e).
[13] It is arguable that *no* concept of philosophical interest can be
defined. See, for example, F. Waismann, "Synthetic-Analytic II,"
Analysis, December 1950; and G. H. von Wright, *Logik, Filosofi
och Språk*, pp.240 ff.

language-games with games in general. What have ball games, card games and board games in common? He says it is no use assuming that because they are classified as games they must have a property in common. They have not. What happens if we look at these games?[14] We find there is no simple property common to all games, but *similar* properties. If we compare a number of games we find the first one has a similar property to the second, and the second another—different—similarity to the third, and so on. Perhaps the first and third also have some points of similarity, but these may be different from the points of similarity between the first and second and between the second and the third. So all members of the class of "games" have, instead of a common defining property, what Wittgenstein calls a "family resemblance."[15]

Consider the resemblances found inside a family. Peter and Paul look similar in profile but not in facial expression, while Paul and John resemble each other in facial expression but not in profile. Peter and John bear no resemblance in facial expression or profile, but have a similar way of speaking. Peter, Paul and John have a "family resemblance," but they have no one specific feature in common.

The word "language" is not the name of a single

[14] "Don't say: 'There *must* be something common or they would not be called "games" '—but *look and see* whether there is anything common to all. . . . To repeat: don't think, but look!" *Philosophical Investigations* §66 (p.31e).
[15] Wittgenstein sums up his point thus: "And the result of this examination is: we see a complicated network of similarities overlapping and crisscrossing: sometimes similarities of detail." Ibid. §66 (p.32e). He goes on in the next paragraph: "I can think of no better expression to characterize these similarities than 'family resemblances'; for the various resemblances between members of a family: build, features, color of eyes, gait, temperament, etc., etc., overlap and crisscross in the same way.—And I shall say, games form a family." Ibid. §67 (p.32e).

phenomenon (as it is said to be in the *Tractatus,* where indeed the assertion is a crucial one); it is the name of the class of an indefinite number of language-games. To talk about *language* as a single and unambiguous phenomenon would be like talking about *the game,* as if there were only *one* game.

Different language-games show a family resemblance, and the number of different language-games is indefinite. Indefinite not only because one can imagine new language-games appearing, but also because the border line of what can be called a language-game is blurred and indistinct—there is no hard edge. The man who stops me by saying, "No admittance," is using a language-game. We should hardly hesitate to say that there is a family resemblance between his speaking this and the board which has the words "No Admittance" painted on it. Nor should we deny a family resemblance between both and a policeman holding up his arm in a gesture made familiar by custom. But what are we to say about a traffic light that changes to red? Or about a barbed-wire fence? Or a white line in the middle of a road? Here we are on the indefinite borderland. No sharp frontier can be discerned between what is and what is not language.

The difference between Wittgenstein's theory of language in the *Philosophical Investigations* and that of the *Tractatus* goes together with a difference of teaching on another question. In the *Tractatus* there is only one language, because language is said to consist of elementary propositions or truth-functions of elementary propositions; and since each of these elementary propositions is a picture of a state of affairs, each has the same logical form as the state of affairs concerned. Since each state of affairs is unique (as it must be in order to be a state of affairs), there can be only one true proposition; from a logical point of view, two propositions about the same state of affairs must be the same proposition in the sense of having the same logical form. To discover the logical forms of the various propositions is to discover the true logical form of the various states of affairs. Philosophy reveals the authentic logical structure of the world. Its task is to analyze sentences so that it can unveil the elementary propositions of which they are truth-functions; and when elementary propositions reveal their logical form they reveal thereby the logical form of the corresponding states of affairs. This argument is repudiated in the *Philosophical Investigations*. First, as we have seen, Wittgenstein repudiates the view that facts can have a logical form. Secondly, he rejects as mistaken the view that states of affairs consist of objects—objects named by the words of which elementary propositions are composed. In the *Tractatus* such objects are conceived of as simple or noncomposite. Now he holds that whether a thing is composite or noncomposite is not in itself an absolute, but something that depends on the language-game.[16] Outside a language-game, apart from a specific linguistic context, it makes no sense to discuss whether an object is or isn't composite.

Imagine a chessboard. In a certain context, one can say that it is made up of black and white *squares* and that each square is simple. In another context, one can say that it is made up of black and white *colors*. These two assertions differ—the word "square" doesn't mean what is meant by the word "color." Which is the correct assertion? This will depend on the context. Neither statement in itself is more correct than the other.[17] If I say that the chessboard is made up of

16 Ibid. §47 (p.21e).
17 "Asking 'Is this object composite?' *outside* a particular language-game is like what a boy once did who had to say whether the verbs in certain sentences were in the active or passive voice,

colored squares, it doesn't follow that in appropriate contexts, a colored square is simple. In one context, it may be said that each square is made up of color and shape; in another that it consists of two rectangles. So Wittgenstein asks: could we not imagine a situation in which the chessboard itself could properly be called a simple object? Now, if the idea of absolutely simple objects is forsaken, one must at the same time abandon the idea that there are simple states of affairs which have a certain logical form. (It will be remembered that a state of affairs was supposed to consist of simple objects and that the logical form was supposed to be determined by the relation between these objects.)

This leads us to a third notable difference between the teachings of Wittgenstein's two books. Language, no longer a picture of reality, is now seen as a tool, and a tool with a rich variety of uses. Different words are like different tools in the toolbox. And just as there is no one use which is the essential use of all tools, there is no one essential use for words and sentences.[18]

4

All in all, the *Philosophical Investigations* gives a radically different account of what philosophy is and does from that which the *Tractatus* gives. The analysis of propositions to set out their correct logical form is no longer relevant, if there is no longer any correct form. The idea of a *correct* form of a proposition is tied to the idea of its depicting a fact. And when there is no longer any logical form of a fact to depict, then there is no standard or norm to establish the correct

and who racked his brains over the question, whether the verb 'to sleep' meant something active or passive." Ibid. §47 (p.22e).
[18] Ibid. §11 (p.6e).

form of a proposition; in other words, the concept "correct form" has lost its meaning. Every sentence is, as Wittgenstein puts it, "in order as it is."[19] The philosopher's task is not to correct the proposition, but to *understand* it. And to understand it means to know not what it pictures, but what it does, what function it has, what purpose it serves, what work it performs. According to the *Tractatus*, a proposition does only one thing—it depicts a fact; but according to *Philosophical Investigations*, sentences do innumerable jobs. It is not easy to say exactly what job a particular sentence does; and perhaps very easy to misunderstand what it is. This is partly because one tends to have in one's mind a prior image of how a particular sentence functions, and it is almost impossible to get rid of this image.

Such, then, is the difference between the teachings on this subject of the *Tractatus* and the *Philosophical Investigations*—according to the earlier work, a proposition may be in a correct or an incorrect form; according to the later work, a proposition has neither a correct nor an incorrect form—it can only be understood or not understood. This may be illustrated by reference to Russell's attempt to translate the statement (1) "The golden mountain does not exist" into the statement (2) "It is false that there is an entity c such that the propositional function 'X is a mountain and of gold' is true if X is c and otherwise false." In the *Tractatus*, Russell's reformulation was regarded as a

[19] "On the one hand, it is clear that every sentence in our language is 'in order as it is.' That is to say, we are not *striving after* an ideal, as if our ordinary vague sentences had not yet got a quite unexceptional sense, and a perfect language awaited construction by us.—On the other hand, it seems clear that where there is sense there must be perfect order.—So there must be perfect order even in the vaguest sentence." Ibid. §98 (p.45e).

correction. Only statement (2) depicts the logical form of reality, and thus only statement (2) is correct. Now, according to the *Philosophical Investigations*, it is wrong to think of statement (2) as a correction of statement (1), for statement (1) is not incorrect in form and does not need correction. On the other hand, Wittgenstein will admit that statement (1) could be misunderstood, indeed that it has been misunderstood.

It is worth remembering that Meinong, among others, rejected the statement "The golden mountain does not exist" as a proposition with a logical subject and a logical predicate. Such theorists fancied it to be analogous to a proposition such as (3), "The golden mountain is 3,000 feet high." And about this last proposition (3), it can be said that the predicate "3,000 feet high" is apropos not of the expression "the golden mountain" but of the subject, the golden mountain itself.

Wittgenstein now holds that Russell's reformulation of statement (1) is not a correction, but an *aid to a better understanding* of that statement; Russell does this by *comparing* (1) with (2), by showing that (1) has the same logical form as (2). Of course, Russell himself did not think of (2) as a fully accurate translation of (1); he thought such a rendering could be provided only by using the symbolic language of *Principia Mathematica*. Wittgenstein, however, will not agree that even the symbolic language of *Principia Mathematica* yields a *correct* translation. According to Wittgenstein, any proposition that serves as a basis of comparison with (1) and so throws light on it has its place in the philosophical investigations of (1). And for this purpose, Russell's statement (2) is not the only useful one. Many other propositions, including less elaborately phrased ones, may serve this end—not only statements showing similarity but also those showing dissimilarity.[20]

What gives point to philosophy is this very fact that propositions and other utterances can be misunderstood. If there were no possibility of misunderstanding, there would be no philosophy. If, like intellectual supermen, we could never misunderstand language, could never go wrong about the job that different sentences do in different contexts, and never mistook one language-game for another, the philosophical problem would be unknown.

Even if we take this claim of Wittgenstein's with some reserve, we may be ready to admit that logical misunderstandings that lead us into philosophical problems can arise from confusing one language-game with another, from supposing that different language-games are one and the same language-game, or from regarding some games (or even one single game, as Wittgenstein himself did in the *Tractatus*) as the only legitimate kind.

Such confusions and oversimplifications, Wittgenstein suggests, are so deeply rooted in our habits of thought that they are not even noticed.[21] The presence of a philosophical problem is symptomatic of a misunderstanding of the logic of language. This is

[20] "Our clear and simple language-games are not preparatory studies for a future regularization of language—as it were first approximations, ignoring friction and air resistance. The language-games are rather set up as *objects of comparison* which are meant to throw light on the facts of our language by way not only of similarities, but also of dissimilarities." Ibid. §130 (p.50e).

[21] "The aspects of things that are most important for us are hidden because of their simplicity and familiarity. (One is unable to notice something—because it is always before one's eyes.) The real foundations of his enquiry do not strike a man at all. Unless *that* fact has at some time struck him.—And this means: we fail to be struck by what, once seen, is most striking and most powerful." Ibid. §129 (p.50e).

not to say that the philosophical problem is of itself a misunderstanding. Indeed, paradoxically, it is, in a sense, a sign of understanding. Philosophical understanding is needed to see the problem caused by a misunderstanding of language. Philosophical problems are bound to arise when one language-game is falsely assumed to be analogous to another language-game; but this is not to say that everybody will see that these problems will arise.

Besides, misunderstandings of the logic of language are not misunderstandings in the ordinary sense of the word. They are not the mistakes that are made on Mondays and Wednesdays but not on Thursdays and Fridays, not the mistakes that we make only when we are tired, or that people of lesser intelligence make more often than those of greater intelligence. They are misunderstandings that originate in the very forms of our language, and which would never be discovered if nobody were able to see the philosophical problems involved.[22] In games like chess and bridge there are rules about what is correct and permissible, and there are rules, again, in deductive systems like mathematics and logic; but language is not in the same situation. There are no analogous rules by which we can determine the use of a word or a sentence in any given context. We know that in logic p and *not* p is a contradiction, and that we can deduce from a contradiction whatever we like. As the field of deduction is limited, it is no contradiction to say in answer to the question "Is he efficient?"—"Both yes and no." No one can reasonably reproach me for such an answer on the grounds that

[22] "One cannot guess how a word functions. One has to *look at* its use and learn from that.

"But the difficulty is to remove the prejudice which stands in the way of doing this. It is not a *stupid* prejudice." Ibid. §340 (p.109e).

one is either efficient or not efficient, that it is impossible to be both efficient and not efficient. Such an answer as mine does not involve me in any ruinous contradiction—it will generally and without difficulty be understood as it should be understood. Only if it was taken as being the same language-game as a deductive logical system, only if I maintained both *p* and *not p*, only then would a reproach be in order. Again, if someone took my answer to be correct, and assumed that I was playing such a deductive logical game, we should end up with metaphysical problems —"The law of contradiction does not apply to human beings."

Thus the way to the solution of a philosophical problem lies in discovering how and why the logic of language has been misunderstood. The philosophical problem is a symptom of something being wrong, and the philosopher's job is to find out what is wrong.[23] The philosophical problem appears to be a problem without a solution precisely because it is not an empirical problem but a problem about the logic of language. One seems to be led to saying something that cannot be right.[24]

The solution of a philosophical problem is reached through a deeper insight into the real function of the sentences under scrutiny, through an understanding of the language-game which is actually being used; hence the task of philosophy becomes purely descriptive, de-

[23] "The philosopher's treatment of a question is like the treatment of an illness." Ibid. §255 (p.91e).

[24] "A simile that has been absorbed into the forms of our language produces a false appearance, and this disquiets us. 'But *this* isn't how it is!' we say. 'Yet *this* is how it has to be.'" Ibid. §112 (p.47e).

"A philosophical problem has the form: 'I don't know my way about.'" Ibid. §123 (p.49e).

scriptive in the sense that it states (or ascertains) how various sentences function.[25]

The kind of misunderstandings which give rise to philosophical problems are, as we have seen, deeply rooted in ordinary thinking; there are features which are hidden not because they are unfamiliar but precisely because they are too familiar. New and unusual things are noticed; everyday occurrences are not. Hence a philosophical discovery does not, as a scientific one so often does, point out something novel and singular (and often meet with skepticism on that account); it points out something which, once seen, seems obvious. For this reason, a philosophical argument is not so often regarded with skepticism and mistrust, but treated rather as a mere truism.[26]

---

[25] "Philosophy may in no way interfere with the actual use of language; it can in the end only describe it. For it cannot give any foundation either. It leaves everything as it is." Ibid. §124 (p.49e).

"When philosophers use a word like 'knowledge,' 'being,' 'object,' 'I,' 'proposition,' 'name,' and try to grasp the *essence* of the thing, one must always ask oneself: is the word ever actually used in this way in the language-game which is its original home?

"What *we* do is to bring words back from their metaphysical to their everyday use." Ibid. §116 (p.48e).

[26] "It was true to say that our considerations could not be scientific ones. It was not of any possible interest to us to find out empirically 'that, contrary to our preconceived ideas, it is possible to think such and such'—whatever that may mean. (The conception of thought as a gaseous medium.) And we may not advance any kind of theory. There must not be anything hypothetical in our considerations. We must do away with all *explanation*, and description alone must take its place. And this description gets its light, that is to say, its purpose, from the philosophical problems. These are, of course, not empirical problems; they are solved, rather, by looking into the workings of our language, and that in such a way as to make us recognize those workings: *in despite of* an urge to misunderstand them. The problems are solved, not by giving new information, but by arranging what we have always

The aim of philosophical reasoning is what Wittgenstein calls complete clarity. It is characteristic of his whole conception of the nature of a philosophical problem that this complete clarity does not lead to the *solution* of the problem, but to its *disappearance*. And to say that it disappears, instead of being solved, is to emphasize that the origin of the philosophical perplexity is an error, or rather a misunderstanding—a misunderstanding of the logical grammar of the sentences concerned. When the misunderstanding has been healed, the source of the problem has not been "solved," it has vanished. Wittgenstein says the problem is like a fly in a fly bottle; and the philosopher's job is to show the fly the way out of the bottle.[27]

This metaphor has a further significance. To show

known. Philosophy is a battle against the bewitchment of our intelligence by means of language." Ibid. §109 (p.47e).

"Philosophy simply puts everything before us, and neither explains nor deduces anything.—Since everything lies open to view, there is nothing to explain. For what is hidden, for example, is of no interest to us." Ibid. §126 (p.50e).

"If one tried to advance *theses* in philosophy, it would never be possible to debate them, because everyone would agree to them." Ibid. §128 (p.50e).

[27] "It is not our aim to refine or complete the system of rules for the use of our words in unheard-of ways.

"For the clarity that we are aiming at is indeed *complete* clarity. But this simply means that the philosophical problems should *completely* disappear.

"The real discovery is the one that makes me capable of stopping doing philosophy when I want to.—The one that gives philosophy peace, so that it is no longer tormented by questions which bring *itself* in question." Ibid. §133 (p.51e).

"The results of philosophy are the uncovering of one or another piece of plain nonsense and of bumps that the understanding has got by running its head up against the limits of language. These bumps make us see the value of the discovery." Ibid. §119 (p.48e).

"What is your aim in philosophy?—To show the fly the way out of the fly bottle." Ibid. §309 (p.103e).

the fly the way out of the fly bottle is not to describe or demonstrate the innumerable directions in which the fly might fly, but simply to show the one that will take it out of the bottle, and that, incidentally, will also be the way that took it into the bottle. Equally, philosophy does not need to describe or demonstrate the many, often countless, uses of a word or an expression, but only the one—or ones—that will make the problem disappear, and this is a matter of revealing the misconception of the logical grammar of the utterance or expression that gave rise to the problem.

5

I have already said a fair amount about Wittgenstein's views on the connection between philosophical problems and misunderstandings about the logic of language. Let us now look at some of the actual philosophical problems he discusses in the *Philosophical Investigations*, and thus turn from his *theory* of the problem to his *treatment* of problems, turn from metaphysical reflection to philosophical investigations, or, in more picturesque Wittgensteinian language, to the therapeutic analysis of specific logical disorders.

Wittgenstein says: "Where our language suggests a body and there is none, there, we should like to say, is a spirit.[28] What he has in mind is this: certain formulations of language lead us to suppose that something exists or that something happens. A statement that something exists will normally be taken to mean that something of a bodily nature exists. If nothing of a bodily nature exists, and we stick to the view that such statements assert the existence of something, we are led to the metaphysical supposition that what

[28] Ibid. §36 (p.18e).

exists must be of a nonbodily or spiritual nature. Thus, in following the supposed logic of language, we are led to talk about spiritual substances.

But this supposed logic is often a misunderstood logic. The problem shows that the functions performed by the words and sentences concerned have been misunderstood. Very often such misunderstanding arises from the mistaken belief that words are names, that the meaning of a word is what it stands for (which leads to the conclusion that if they do not refer to anything they are meaningless, and that all meaningful words and sentences must refer to something).

Now, there are many verbs that refer to things that happen or to things we do physically—"to hurry," "to run," "to speak," "to work," "to eat," and so forth. These are verbs referring to bodily activities. Then there are all those verbs which, with apparently equal force, refer to processes or activities that are *not* bodily activities—"to wish," "to decide," "to understand," and so on. Wittgenstein's remark is relevant to the use of these verbs. The language *seems* to refer to a bodily activity; and when there is no bodily activity, we are led to talk about some spiritual or incorporeal activity instead. For example, we say, "Now I understand," or, "Now I see it." We think of such expressions as belonging to the same logical type as expressions referring to physical activities or processes. We misunderstand the function which the words perform and so get led into philosophical problems about "mental acts" and so forth.[29]

---

[29] "How does the philosophical problem about mental processes and states and about behaviorism arise?—The first step is the one that altogether escapes notice. We talk of processes and states and leave their nature undecided. Sometime, perhaps, we shall know more about them, we think. But that is just what commits us to a particular way of looking at this matter. For we have a definite concept of what it means to know a process better. (The decisive movement in the conjuring trick has been made, and it is the very

Suppose I treat the expression "Now I understand" as a *report*—a report on my having understood something or other. The obvious question arises: what does it report? And the obvious answer is: it reports the very understanding that occurred, a report of the flash of understanding that seems to constitute the understanding itself; a report of the occurrence of a definite mental act, namely, that of understanding.

Such a view leads us into difficulties. Let us suppose that there *is* such a mental act, and that the sentence "Now I understand" is a report of its occurrence. This means that I must be able to observe such mental acts, for otherwise I could not report them. Wittgenstein now attempts to establish the following points: (1) There is no single mental act that occurs every time I begin to realize something or every time I understand. (2) Even if there were such a single mental act, observable every time I begin to realize something, or every time I understand, then it would still be wrong to call it an act of understanding. (3) If the expression "Now I understand" is treated as a report, it entails the very odd suggestion that such an utterance is a report of something that has never been observed.[30]

---

one that we thought quite innocent.)—And now the analogy which was to make us understand our thoughts falls to pieces. So we have to deny the yet uncomprehended process in the yet unexplored medium. And now it looks as if we had denied mental processes. And naturally we don't want to deny them." Ibid. §308 (p.103e).

[30] "We are trying to get hold of the mental process of understanding which seems to be hidden behind these coarser, and therefore more readily visible accompaniments. But we do not succeed; or rather it does not get us as far as a real attempt. For even supposing that I had found something that happened in all those cases of understanding—why should *it* be the understanding? And how can the process of understanding have been hidden, when I said, 'Now I understand,' *because* I understood?! And if I say it is hidden—then how do I know what I have to look for? I am in a muddle." Ibid. §153 (p.60e).

Wittgenstein gives the following example: A writes down a series of numbers following a specific system. B, watching A write them down, tries to discover the rule he is following. At a certain moment he grasps it, whereupon he exclaims, for example, "Now I understand," or, "Now I know how to go on." What are his reasons for saying this? Suppose the series of numbers is 1, 5, 11, 19, 29. After the figure 29 has been written down, B says he knows now how to go on. While A was writing, B was trying out various algebraic formulas on the numbers. After the figure 19 has been written down, B speculates as to whether the formula $a_n = n^2 + n - 1$ is the one he is looking for. If so, the next number in the series will be 29; and when A writes this figure, B thinks he has discovered the rule. But this is only one method, and by no means the only possible one. B, while watching A write out the numbers, may have had many different ideas, and may perhaps have finally noticed that the difference between the numbers was 4, 6, 8, 10, and so have announced that he knew how to go on.[31]

But whatever thoughts or ideas B had, none of them can be said to constitute understanding itself. Even if it could be proved that one single thought or idea is always present when a man understands something, this would still differ from understanding. Understanding, in the example we have just considered, cannot be identified with B's thinking of the formula $a_n = n^2 + n - 1$. For he may well have come to think of this without having understood the rule underlying the series of numbers which A had written down. He may think of it in the sense of seeing it in his mind's eye (as we see a word spelled out when we try to imagine it with closed eyes), and he could do this without con-

[31] Ibid. §151 (p.59).

necting it with anything and without knowing the meaning or use of it. And what is true of the formula $a_n = n^2 + n - 1$ applies equally to anything else that B might think of or imagine.[32] It might even be said that although one had a particular idea that could be called an "idea of understanding," it would be logically permissible to ask if one had understood or misunderstood this idea.

In other words, we have been led to this conclusion: if an expression like "Now I understand" is taken as a *report* (or a description) of a mental act of understanding, we must acknowledge that it cannot be a report (or description) of anything. And this indicates that it is a misunderstanding of the logic of such expressions to regard them as reports (or descriptions). There are further reasons for saying this. Suppose, in the example given, B says, "Now I understand," and this statement is a report of a mental event, then the statement would be correct if, and only if, the mental event were actually experienced. In this case, B would be justified in maintaining that he had understood even though he could not continue the series of numbers. And correspondingly, if he were able to continue the series of numbers, but had not experienced any mental event, then he would have no right to say he had understood.

It would be no more correct to regard it as a matter of experience, or to hold that one had empirical evi-

[32] "But are the processes which I have described here *understanding?*

" 'B understands the principle of the series' surely doesn't mean simply: the formula 'a_n = etc.' occurs to B. For it is perfectly imaginable that the formula should occur to him and that he should nevertheless not understand. 'He understands' must have more in it than: the formula occurs to him. And equally, more than any of those more or less characteristic *accompaniments* or manifestations of understanding." Ibid. §152 (p.60e).

dence for saying that every time one had the idea of understanding, or experienced the supposed mental event of understanding, it meant that one was able to act with understanding. For if this were so, then to say, "Now I understand," would be the same as to say, "I have empirical grounds for believing that I shall be able to act correctly."[33]

But if the statement in question is not a report (or a description) of an act of understanding or a mental process—and such is the conclusion we have reached—how then should it be regarded? It is something that cannot be said *until* one has understood. Notice, this means when one *has understood,* and not (as might be fancied) when one *understands.* The simple reason is that one must either have already understood or not yet understood. The verb "to understand" has this feature in common with several other verbs. To begin is to have begun; to see is to have seen; to win is to have won. No situation can be sensibly described by saying that it is beginning but has not begun; one cannot say that a man is seeing but has not yet seen; or that he is understanding but has not yet understood.[34]

Assuredly, we use phrases like "He is on the point of seeing," or "It is dawning on him." And we speak like this precisely in those cases where a man has not yet quite seen or understood, but is getting close to seeing or understanding. But to be close to a goal is not to be there.

[33] "And now one might think that the sentence 'I can go on' meant 'I have an experience which I know empirically to lead to the continuation of the series.' But does B mean that when he says he can go on? Does that sentence come to his mind, or is he ready to produce it in explanation of what he meant?" Ibid. §179 (p.72e).

[34] "Try not to think of understanding as a 'mental process' at all—for *that* is the expression which confuses you." Ibid. §154 (p.61e).

I say, "Now I understand," when I have already understood. In Wittgenstein's words it is a "signal" that I can go on—or "a glad start."[35] In many ways it is no more a report (or description) than is the exclamation "Hurrah!" If I am struggling with a difficult job, untying a knot, searching for something I've lost, for example, I may at the moment when I succeed exclaim—"That's it!" or "Done it!" or "Hurrah!" In this context, all these exclamations belong to the same logical category (the same part of the same language-game). Nobody would consider "Hurrah" or "That's it" or "Done it" in this context as reports or descriptions. And yet such utterances as "Now I understand," or "Now I know how to go on," belong to the same logical category.

Now, exclamations like "Hurrah" and "That's it" cannot be true or false in the sense that propositions can be—but they can be *justified*. One might, for instance, afterward say, "It was too early for me to say 'Hurrah' or 'I thought I had it.'" My joy or relief at having succeeded may be expressed in various exclamations; but it may rest on a false foundation and therefore be unjustified. But it would be meaningless to say that the joy or relief (or the corresponding exclamation) was false. The same applies to the sentence "Now I understand." It cannot be true or false, but it may be justified or unjustified. Indeed, if this were not so, we could not speak of "misunderstanding." To misunderstand is to believe, fallaciously, that one has understood. Then a situation arises when we should

[35] "It would be quite misleading in this last case, for instance, to call the words a 'description of a mental state.'—One might rather call them a 'signal,' and we judge whether it was rightly employed by what he goes on to do." Ibid. §180 (p.73e).
"'Now I know how to go on!' is an exclamation: it corresponds to instinctive sounds, a glad start." Ibid. §323 (p.105e).

say, "When I said I understood, I thought I had, but now it seems that I was mistaken." The evidence of its being a mistake is found in what one does and says, or perhaps in what one doesn't do or say. Even so, this does not mean that the claim "Now I understand," or "Now I know how to go on," must have been unjustified if I get stuck or go on and make a mistake. For there are situations when it would be permissible to say, "When I said I understood I really did understand, but now I seem to have forgotten it."[36]

But what is the justification for maintaining that at one moment one understood something and the next moment forgot it? Does it not consist in an appeal to that very flash of understanding, the existence of which Wittgenstein denies? Here it is important to distinguish between cause and justification. The cause of B's exclamation, "Now I understand," was that he thought of the formula $a_n = n^2 + n - 1$, and that the application of it produced the right number, or that he spotted that the difference between the numbers A wrote down was 4, 6, 8 and 10, respectively. Or perhaps there was no other cause than his immediate recognition[37] of the series of numbers, or his instant realization that he knew how to go on[38] when he had seen the first few numbers A wrote down.

But no matter what images may have been in B's mind, and no matter what the cause, or better, the

---

[36] Ibid. §181–82 (p.73e), and §323 (pp.105–6e).

[37] "Or he watches and says, 'Yes, I know *that* series'—and continues it, just as he would have done if A had written down the series 1 3 5 7 9." Ibid. §151 (p.60e).

[38] "We can also imagine the case where nothing at all occurred in B's mind except that he suddenly said, 'Now I know how to go on'—perhaps with a feeling of relief; and that he did in fact go on working out the series without using the formula. And in this case, too, we should say—in certain circumstances—that he did know how to go on." Ibid. §179 (p.73e).

occasion of his exclamation "Now I understand," it has nothing to do with its justification. That can be based only on B's ability to show he has understood by a certain performance—a performance already begun with what Wittgenstein calls "the glad start." It may still be justified even though the performance goes wrong, and in this case, the matter will be determined by finding out the cause of what has gone wrong or got stuck in the performance. If, for example, one can truly say that one has forgotten what one knew a little while ago, then it can be reasonably held that one did really understand even though one no longer understands. On the other hand, if someone in B's position said he *believed* he could go on with the series, but in fact could not go on, then we must say that in this case, he believed he had understood but had not understood.[39]

6

A special class of words refers to sensations—pain, itching, burning, pricking and so on—and such phenomena might be, and often have been, called "inner" or "private" events. Being so named, they are set apart from external or public phenomena. Tables and chairs are external and publicly observable bodies—they exist in space, and everyone can see and feel them. But a sensation is not in space as a table is in space, so it is called "inner," and it is not experienced by anyone except myself, so it is called "private." These so-called inner, private experiences are designated by particular words, and the words come to be regarded as names,

[39] "Here there are cases in which I should say, 'When I said I know how to go on, I *did* know.' One will say that if, for example, an unforeseen interruption occurs. What is unforeseen must not simply be that I got stuck." Ibid. §323 (p.105e).

names which in use give rise to assertions about reports (or descriptions) of the sensations concerned. And a language which thus asserts, reports or describes these inner, private sensations is called a private language.

How do we learn this language? Now, what Wittgenstein wants to show is that such a private language does not exist, indeed, that it could not exist, that it is a logical impossibility. What he claims is that the language we use when we talk about our sensations is not a naming language-game, not a language which names inner and private sensations. Wittgenstein tries to prove the logical impossibility of such a language in this way: suppose I experience a certain sensation and decide to name it. I call it "E."[40] Now I also decide to write down "E" in my diary every time I have the sensation "E." "E" must in this case be regarded as a name and not as a description (as, for example, piercing, pricking, burning or oppressive).[41] The sensation can be defined only ostensively. I notice a sensation, I concentrate—more or less—my attention on it, and so, as it were, decide to name it "E." To have named the sensation means, among other things, that the next time I become aware of the same sensation I shall call it "E" and write that word in my diary.

Now suppose that some time after I have named the sensation, I experience it again and accordingly write down "E." Can this be justified? Noticing the sensa-

[40] Ibid. §258 (p.92e). The "E" comes from the German for "sensation," "*Empfindung*."
[41] Personally I must add that I doubt whether sensations exist which cannot in principle be characterized or described by means of just such expressions as piercing, burning or oppressive, i.e., expressions which indicate the external causes of the sensation. In my article, "Remarks on the Concept of Sensations," I have tried to show that no sensations are known that cannot be so characterized. See *The Journal of Philosophy*, Vol. LVI, No. 3, 1959.

tion, I concentrate my attention on it, and identify it as "E," I recognize it as the sensation I experienced before and named "E." Now this name "E" is correctly applied only if I have identified the sensation correctly. And by writing down "E" I assert that I have identified it correctly. But to speak of correctness is to imply the existence of a criterion of correctness. If there were no such criterion it would be absurd to speak of correctness. If, for example, I say that today is Tuesday, there must, in principle at any rate, be some test to establish whether today is Tuesday and not Monday or Thursday. If there is no way of testing it, the assertion makes no sense—the word "Tuesday" could perform no function in the language.

So what is the criterion for the sensation I have today and call "E" being the same as the one I had the other day and also called "E"? All I can say if I am asked is that it *seems to me* to be so, I think it is, or some such words. We are used to giving answers of this kind in innumerable situations, for innumerable situations arise in which such answers are justified. To questions such as, "Is the man who is here the same man who was here the other day?" "Is the tune you are playing the same as the one you played yesterday?" "Is he making the same speech as he made last year?"—to all such questions, it may be right to answer, "I think so," "It seems to me that it is so," and so forth. And in each of these cases there is—in principle at least—some way of finding out whether what seems to be the case *is* the case. There are various ways of ascertaining whether it really was the same man, the same tune, or the same speech, but my impression that it is, is not itself a criterion. My having the belief or the impression that a thing is the case is not a method of testing that it is the case. But it may act as a stimulus or incentive to verify something, and it may give a hint as to how to do so and what to look for. To fancy that something is so is not to have ascertained anything, but perhaps it may serve to prompt one to ascertain something.

Now, when we turn to the question whether what seems to be the same is not a man or a tune or a speech but a sensation, then we are faced with a situation where there are no methods for ascertaining whether what seems to be the same is really the same. Why are there no such methods? It is not because they cannot be found, or because one's situation cuts one off from their use. The reason is of a logical kind. We could not conceive of a method of ascertaining whether one sensation was the same as another felt at an earlier time. For there is nothing for me to go by except that the sensation *seems* to me to be the same. This means there is no difference between the two statements "It is the same sensation that I had before," and "It is not the same sensation that I had before," or, what comes to the same thing, "This is sensation E," and "This is not sensation E." There is no difference, for no criterion of truth can be applied to them. And a proposition so formulated that it makes no difference whether it is true or false is not a proposition at all.

Thus the sign "E" is no name. It was incorrectly taken for a name. A name without a criterion for its proper use, for which, in other words, no rules exist, is not a name. It is not part of any language-game; it has no function; it has no task to perform.

Perhaps someone will suggest that *memory* must explain why the sensation appears to be the same sensation that I had the other day. *I remember* the sensation I had then, and therefore I can say that the sensation I am having now is the same. After all, it is not absurd to have some confidence in what one thinks one remembers. We often demonstrate such confidence. I remember that the train leaves at 10 A.M.; and as I rely on my memory, I don't look up the timetable. However, the decisive point in this case is that a criterion *exists* as to whether my memory is sound or unsound. If the timetable indicates that the train leaves at 10 A.M., then my memory is correct; but if the timetable indicates another hour, my memory is incorrect. In the case of remembering a sensation, no such criterion exists. There is nothing to which I can appeal to validate my memory. Wittgenstein gives the example of someone who wants to translate a word from one language into another, but a language which is not spoken and in which no dictionary exists, apart from an imaginary dictionary. You imagine a dictionary and then look up the word in its pages. Then in what sense would it be possible to speak of a correct or incorrect translation? It would make sense only if the imaginary dictionary could itself be checked, but this *ex hypothesi* is out of the question.[42]

What Wittgenstein has shown (or believes that he

[42] "Let us imagine a table (something like a dictionary) that exists only in our imagination. A dictionary can be used to justify the translation of a word X by a word Y. But are we also to call it justification if such a table is to be looked up only in the imagination? 'Well, yes, then it is a subjective justification.'—But justification consists in appealing to something independent. 'But surely I can appeal from one memory to another. For example, I don't know if I have remembered the time of departure of a train right, and to check it I call to mind how the page of the timetable looked. Isn't it the same here?' No; for this process has got to produce a memory which is actually *correct*. If the mental image of the timetable could not itself be *tested* for correctness, how could it confirm the correctness of the first memory? (As if someone were to buy several copies of the morning paper to assure himself that what was said was true.)

"Looking up a table in the imagination is no more looking up a table than the image of the result of an imaginary experiment is the result of an experiment." *Philosophical Investigations* §265 (pp.93e–94e).

has shown) by this attack on private language is not that we are all talking nonsense when we speak of our sensations, but, on the contrary, that such talk, or such a language-game, must not be taken as a language containing names of sensations. If the sign "E" is read as the name of a sensation, but a name which is neither a description nor any other characterization of the sensation it names, then "E" does not fulfill the conditions necessary for any sign to function as a name. What is named must be identifiable. If this cannot be done, the logical conditions for naming are not being satisfied.

Nevertheless, the fact remains that we can, and do, talk about our sensations; so the question remains, if we are not naming sensations, what are we doing? Well, let us imagine we are speaking of a sensation with which a certain type of behavior is connected. This will be the case where, for example, a painful sensation is concerned. Is our mentioning the pain a naming or description of the behavior? Clearly not. When I want a pain to end, it is not my behavior that I want to end. I take an aspirin as a remedy against certain pain, not against certain behavior. Then is the behavior to be regarded as a symptom of the pain, as an external sign by means of which I identify the pain? It is plainly no such thing. When I say I have a pain, it is not an inductive conclusion. I do not infer it from my behavior. I do not verify my claim that I have a pain by observing what I say and do. But why must an expression such as "I have a pain" be an assertion about a sensation? To discover the meaning of a statement is not to discover what it may describe or refer to, but to discover its use. And a good method for finding out how a certain expression is used in certain situations and for certain purposes is to investigate how one would set about teaching someone its use, or how we actually learn it ourselves. It is, however, by no means easy to find out how we actually learn to use words like "pain," or, what is the same thing, how we come to understand what the words mean.

Consider the following suggestion: I learn what the word "pain" means by having a pain myself. Certain behavior is connected with the pain. When I have a pain and exhibit this behavior, I am told that what I feel and what causes the behavior is pain. But this cannot be a true explanation of how I learn the meaning of the word. For if I learn it from my behavior, then the expression "I have a pain" becomes a conclusion. "Ow!" I exclaim, and pull a face, so I must have a pain? This is absurd. If I do not learn it from my behavior, then perhaps I learn it in this way: the first time that I learn that the sensation I am feeling is called "pain," I concentrate my attention on it and so come to think I have learned the meaning of pain. But this is the same as saying that I know what the word "pain" means as a result of comparing subsequent sensations with this sensation; and this leads to the same difficulty as before—we do not know what counts as having identified a sensation correctly, so it is meaningless to speak of the correct or incorrect use of the word.

To regard the utterance "I have a pain" as an assertion about a sensation leads us into difficulties. And, according to Wittgenstein, the way out of these difficulties is to admit that it is a misunderstanding to treat the utterance as an assertion; and then to go on to see that using this expression is not the language-game we supposed, but another, very different language-game. What kind of language-game is it in reality? Wittgenstein answers in these terms: when a child in a given situation has a pain and shows pain-behavior, it learns through the comments and questions of adults to call it a pain. "It stings!" "It hurts!" "Does it hurt?" "Do you have a pain?" and so forth. This reveals—and here we have the crucial point for Wittgenstein—that the utterance "I have a pain" is not used as an assertion about a pain-sensation, nor as an assertion or description of pain-behavior, but as part, even though a part acquired by habit, of the pain-behavior itself.[43] On this analysis of "I have a pain" the difficulties we have discussed can be avoided. At the same time, light has been thrown on other logical peculiarities of this utterance.

When any of us makes an assertion, that assertion may be false, not only in the sense that one wishes to deceive people, but also in the sense that one may be mistaken. The most simple assertions can sometimes be false. Assertions such as "I see there is a table in the room" are perhaps most often true, but they can be false. Not even such an assertion as "I see a red spot" is necessarily true. It is quite possible that owing to some special circumstances, I misjudge the color. There is no logical absurdity in remarks such as "I was sure I saw that the spot was red, but now I see that the color isn't red, but bronze, so I was obviously mistaken." On the other hand, it would be a logical absurdity to say, "I was sure I had a severe dull pain, but

[43] "How do words *refer* to sensations? There doesn't seem to be any problem here; don't we talk about sensations every day, and give them names? But how is the connection between the name and the thing named set up? The question is the same as, how does a human being learn the meaning of the names of sensations?—of the word 'pain,' for example? Here is one possibility—words are connected with the primitive, the natural expressions of the sensations, and used in their place. A child has hurt himself and he cries; and the adults talk to him and teach him exclamations, and later sentences. They teach the child new pain-behavior.

"So you are saying that the word 'pain' really means crying? On the contrary, the verbal expression of pain replaces crying and does not describe it." Ibid. §244 (p.89e).

98

now I believe that the sensation was a sharp itching, so I was obviously mistaken."

This leads us to another logical peculiarity. Any assertion is either known or supposed to be true. Hence one must be able to answer questions as to how one knows its truth. If I say "There is a red spot on the wall," I can be asked how I know it; and if I say "I see a red spot on the wall," I can be asked if I am sure I am seeing it correctly, and I can be asked to look at it more closely. But if I say I am in great pain, it would be a logical absurdity to ask how I know it, or believe it, or to ask me whether I am sure; and I could not, except as a joke, be asked to pay more attention to the sensation to make sure that it is not perhaps an itch. Now, it seems to be a logical condition of knowing or believing an assertion to be true that questions of this kind can be asked. If such questions cannot be put, then we cannot be said when to know or believe that which has been said is true, in other words, that the utterance is an assertion. This would therefore seem to show that "I am in great pain" is not an assertion, not anything that I can be said to *know* to be true.[44]

These logical oddities can be clarified if they are

[44] "In what sense are my sensations *private?*—Well, only I can know whether I am really in pain; another person can only surmise it.—In one way this is wrong, and in another nonsense. If we are using the word 'to know' as it is normally used (and how else are we to use it?), then other people very often know when I am in pain.—Yes, but all the same not with the certainty with which I know it myself! It can't be said of me at all (except perhaps as a joke) that I *know* I am in pain. What is it supposed to mean—except perhaps that I *am* in pain.

"Other people cannot be said to learn of my sensations *only* from my behavior, for *I* cannot be said to learn of them. I *have* them.

"The truth is: it makes sense to say about other people that they doubt whether I am in pain; but not to say it about myself." Ibid. §246 (p.89^e).

seen in the light of Wittgenstein's argument that the utterance "I am in pain" is not an assertion but part of pain-behavior. It neither describes the pain nor describes the pain-behavior; it replaces a part of the pain-behavior (the cry). This shows why it does not make sense to say I was mistaken when I believed I had a pain, but had only an itch. It would be equally absurd, and absurd for the same reason, as saying that it was a mistake for me to cry "Ow!" or wince, instead of scratching myself. For the same reason, again, I cannot answer questions about how I know I am in pain, and cannot be urged to pay more attention to confirm that I am not mistaken; I cannot be asked how I know I am right to cry "Ow!" or be urged to investigate more closely and see if I was right to wince rather than scratch.

7

In the *Philosophical Investigations,* Wittgenstein touches on many different philosophical problems. One leads on to another, or is examined in the light of another, and, just as often, examined in the light of a third problem. These in turn are examined in the light of further problems. Thus one is taken by a complicated series of crisscross journeys through an ever wider field of thought, an adventure which yields what Wittgenstein calls a collection of landscape sketches, sketches that in the end combine to provide an overall panorama of the whole terrain. He compares his own book to an album.[45]

[45] "The thoughts which I publish in what follows are the precipitate of philosophical investigations which have occupied me for the past sixteen years. . . . I have written down all these thoughts as *remarks,* short paragraphs, of which there is sometimes a fairly long chain about the same subject, while I some-

We have now looked at the central points Wittgenstein makes in the *Philosophical Investigations*. His conception of language as so many language-games (rather than a picture of facts); his theory that language can serve many different purposes—describing, commanding, asking, appointing, etc., as well as naming—and that the meaning of a word is governed by the language-game in which it figures; his argument that philosophical problems are rooted in misunderstandings of the type of language-game in which a particular word occurs: all this, as we have seen, leads to his claim that the proper business of philosophy is to remove these misunderstandings by elucidating the correct language-game in which such words are used.

We have also noted that these central ideas of Wittgenstein are relevant to two far-reaching problems, or, more precisely, to two sets of far-reaching problems, for each is related to many others. Problems that stem from the expression "Now I understand" arise, according to Wittgenstein, from a mistaken belief that this expression describes or reports something, and so from mistaking the language-game to which (according to Wittgenstein) the expression really belongs. This mis-

---

times make a sudden change, jumping from one topic to another. . . . And this was, of course, connected with the very nature of the investigation. For this compels us to travel over a very wide field of thought crisscross in every direction.—The philosophical remarks in this book are, as it were, a number of sketches of landscapes which were made in the course of these long and involved journeyings.

"The same, or almost the same points are always being approached afresh from different directions, and new sketches made. Very many of these were badly drawn or uncharacteristic, marked by all the defects of a weak draughtsman. And when they were rejected, a number of tolerable ones were left, which now had to be arranged and sometimes cut down, so that if you looked at them you could get a picture of the landscape.—Thus this book is really only an album." Ibid. (p.IXe).

understanding arises from a theory of meaning according to which the meaning of a sentence is what it refers to. The expression "I have a pain" yields similar problems if it is taken (as it was taken by theorists before Wittgenstein) as an assertion naming a sensation and not (as Wittgenstein argues) as a form of acquired pain-behavior.

It is a very common fallacy that sentences which are *not* assertions, reports or descriptions *are* assertions, reports or descriptions.[46] And this mistake goes together with the equally common fallacy of taking the meaning of a sentence to be what it refers to rather than the way it is used.

Although such errors still prevail, one has only to glance at the philosophy going on nowadays, at least in the Anglo-Saxon world, to see that it has been decisively, though not of course exclusively, influenced by Wittgenstein's teaching. To put it rather crudely, one might say that two schools have dominated the academic philosophers of the past twenty years: first logical positivism, and second the "analytic" philosophy originating in England, mainly at Cambridge and Oxford. Curiously enough, *both* these movements were inspired by Wittgenstein, the one by the earlier Wittgenstein of the *Tractatus*, the other by the later Wittgenstein of the *Philosophical Investigations*. And just as the Wittgenstein of the *Tractatus* was conquered by the Wittgenstein of the *Philosophical Investigations*, so one could say that logical positivism is being, if not conquered, at any rate outdistanced, and forced into retreat, by the teachings of the later Wittgenstein that have been developed at Cambridge and Oxford.

[46] A fallacy common enough to warrant a name. John Austin called it "the descriptive fallacy" that is "so common a philosophy." See his paper, "Other Minds," in *Logic and Language*, Second Series, ed. A. G. N. Flew, p.146.

In the past fifteen or twenty years, important things have happened in philosophy. Where darkness ruled before, it now seems that one can not only hope for light but also sense its approach, and even, here and there, catch a glimpse of it. It is worth noting that these gains have often been produced through the close and detailed investigations of a single expression or group of related expressions, and that the decisive point—that at which we came to see things in a new light and in a new way—has nearly always been a demonstration of the way the expressions concerned have been misunderstood, or, in Wittgenstein's terms, have been supposed to belong to the wrong language-game. All this is due to Wittgenstein's teaching; and in the chapter that follows, I shall give some examples of the work that has been done by a few of the English philosophers who have been influenced by him.

V

Contemporary Philosophical
Investigations

1

One of the most influential philosophy books that has appeared since the war is *The Concept of Mind* by Gilbert Ryle, Waynflete Professor of Metaphysics at Oxford.[1] It was published in 1949, four years before the *Philosophical Investigations,* and it is not Wittgensteinian in style or outlook, although there is no conflict on essential points; but it is typically Wittgensteinian in that it treats philosophical problems as the consequence of a misunderstanding of the logic of concepts.

[1] Gilbert Ryle (b.1900): editor of *Mind;* author of *The Concept of Mind, Dilemmas,* etc.

Where Wittgenstein speaks of language-games, Ryle speaks of "categories." What Ryle has in mind is this: Suppose I cut the stalk of an apple on a tree, then the following statements can be made: (1) An apple is hanging on a tree (2) The apple is subject to the law of gravity (3) I cut its stalk (4) The apple falls to the ground because of the law of gravity (5) The apple falls to the ground because its stalk is cut.

Take sentence (3) first. This can be read as a report of what I am doing, a statement of something that happens. Such a sentence, thus used to report an occurrence, is a categorical statement. It implies the logical possibility of asking certain questions; not that the answers are necessarily known, but that they could be known. Sentence (3) implies, among other things, that one can ask where I cut the stalk, when it happened and how long it took.

Next, let us look at sentence (2). That an apple is subject to the law of gravity cannot meaningfully be said to occur at a definite moment or to have taken a long or short time. An apple is subject to the law of gravity whether it is on a tree, or in a bowl, or falling to the ground. Its being subject to this law is no more a *happening* than the fact that this paper is inflammable. Paper is inflammable whether it is lying on the desk or burning in the grate. Hence to say that the apple is subject to the law of gravity is not to report any occurrence. So it makes no sense to ask when it occurred. Thus (2) is not a categorical, but a *hypothetical* statement. What (2) asserts is that *if* for some reason an apple is not held up, it will fall in accordance with the law of gravity. Hence (2) has a function altogether different from (3); (2) can be considered a rule of inference by means of which one can say what will happen (that the apple will fall) if certain other things happen (that the apple ceases to be held up);

and one can explain what happens by showing that it happens in accordance with this rule. (2) and (3) are logically different statements—they belong to different logical categories. To treat (2) as if it belonged to the same logical category as (3) would commit one to answering senseless questions; it is to make a category mistake which leads to absurdities.

If (2) and (3) belong to different categories, so do (4) and (5). In (4) it is stated that the apple falls because of gravity, and in (5) that it falls because its stalk has been cut. These two uses of "because of" belong to two different categories; and to suppose that they belong to the same one is again to make a category mistake. In (5) the fall of the apple is explained in terms of a cause; in (4) in terms of a law. To be a cause something must happen, occur, take place. The cause of a billiard ball's rolling is that another ball has struck it. The lightning was the cause of the house catching fire, and the cutting of the stalk was the cause of the apple falling. But the law of gravity is not an event, it does not happen; so it makes no sense to call it a cause. To explain the apple's falling by referring to the law of gravity is to explain it in terms of a rule. Thus the relationship between (4) and (5) is this: (5) explains in terms of the cause, the cutting of the stalk. But, in this case, the cutting of the stalk can be the cause of the apple's falling only if (4) is correct. To say that something is a cause is to say, *inter alia,* that there is a rule of inference (a law) in the light of which one is justified in making an inference from certain occurrences to certain other occurrences, and the event in question is one of that class to which this rule of inference can be applied. Without such rules of inference, or laws, the word "cause" would have no meaning.

Thus, while (2) is a hypothetical statement, and

(3) and (5) are categorical statements, (4) is neither, or, more precisely, both. It is categorical in that it reports that the apple falls, and hypothetical in that it explains this event by means of a rule of inference. The rule of inference and the report are, so to speak, built into the same statement. Ryle calls such statements "semi-hypothetical" or "mongrel-categorical."[2]

Ryle's subject in *The Concept of Mind* is one of the classical problems of philosophy. Even though it did not originate with Descartes—for it is a much older problem—one might say that Descartes first gave it a modern formulation. And although the Cartesian theory leads to insurmountable difficulties, it has nevertheless captured our minds—it has given us our idea of how things must be.[3] Broadly speaking, the Cartesian theory is this: man is made up of two entities, a body and a mind; these two entities interact, so that some events in the one may be caused by events in the other. Thus, according to circumstances, we act from anger, prudence, indulgence, envy, vanity, sorrow, and so forth. Or we are angry, prudent, indulgent, envious, vain, sorrowful, and the rest. To explain actions by means of mental concepts—"He did it because he was angry," "He did it out of shrewdness," "His conduct was dictated by envy," etc.—to speak thus, according to the Cartesian theory, is to have given a causal explanation. The causes invoked are mental processes. I have the feeling called envy, and this feeling is the cause of my conduct. Or my intelligence works out what would be the most profitable thing for me to do, and these mental processes are the causes of my subsequent be-

[2] *The Concept of Mind*, p.141.
[3] Compare Wittgenstein's remark: "A simile that has been absorbed into the forms of our language produces a false appearance, and this disquiets us. 'But *this* isn't how it is!' we say. 'Yet *this* is how it has to *be*.'" *Philosophical Investigations* §112 (p.47e).

havior. Thus a man whose actions are explained by means of mental concepts is a being in whom two things take place: the physical action and the mental process. And while the physical actions can be discovered by other people, mental processes can be observed only by the person who experiences them. Physical actions are public and occur in space, mental processes are private and do not occur in space. Mental events are events of a peculiar, even a mystical kind, and how they can bring about physical events is a problem that has continued to worry philosophers since Descartes. It is puzzling to speak of mental events as internal, and puzzling to call the physical actions external. To call something internal is to say it is inside something, and what is external is outside something. But what is this "something"? The external, in this context, is still external whether it is inside my own body or outside. Hence, in this context, "internal" cannot mean "inside" anything; the word cannot have its ordinary meaning, and, indeed, it is difficult, nay, impossible to say what meaning it has at all. And so long as no meaning can be ascribed to the word "internal," none can be ascribed to the word "external" either.

It is equally puzzling how one person can make any inference about the state, or even the existence, of another person's mind. For *ex hypothesi* one can observe only what goes on in one's own mind. The belief that states of mind or mental events are experienced by others is an inference based on analogy from one's own inner experience. But if this inference is to be better than a mere guess, it must have empirical support; there must have been cases when this inference was confirmed. Now, according to the Cartesian theory, this is impossible. It has never been and never will be possible to verify an inference from analogy;

such inferences are therefore no better than guesses.[4]

Such are the difficulties which arise within the conceptual scheme or framework of Cartesian theory. And it is this conceptual framework which Ryle attacks. Ryle claims that it is a logical error to explain people's actions in Cartesian terms. It is a "category mistake." That is to say, it is not the kind of mistake that can be corrected by psychology. The Cartesian conceptual apparatus does not make it possible for us to predict what results a particular psychological experiment should, or should not, produce, so experiments can neither confirm nor refute it. But the conceptual scheme shapes our interpretation of what is shown by the experiments, and conditions our explanations of them. If the conceptual framework is incorrect, the understanding becomes misunderstanding, and the explanations sham explanations.

In brief, according to Ryle, the Cartesian category mistake is to confuse cause and law, or to classify as categorical statements what are in fact hypothetical or semi-hypothetical statements, or to classify as assertions, sentences that actually function as inference rules.

Consider the sentence: "His action was prompted by vanity." This is a sentence that can in certain circumstances be used correctly. But this is not to say it cannot be misunderstood. Indeed, one may suggest that being formulated as it is, it is apt to be misunderstood. The use of the word "prompted" suggests a causal relation, the feeling of vanity being a mental event causing the physical action, in the same way that cutting the stalk of the apple causes the apple to fall. The statement is thus treated as one containing two categorical statements, one reporting a mental

[4] Ryle, op. cit., pp.14 ff. and pp.52 ff.

event, the so-called feeling of vanity, and the other reporting the actions caused by this feeling. This is a
mistake. In truth, the statement is semi-hypothetical
in the same way as the statement "The apple falls because of the law of gravity" is semi-hypothetical. To
say that his action is prompted by vanity is to explain
it by referring to a trait of character, namely, vanity.
To say a man is vain is to make a hypothetical statement, just as it is when one says that an apple is subject to the law of gravity. If I say a man is vain, I do
not say he is experiencing a particular feeling called
vanity more or less frequently or at intervals or all the
time.[5] I do not say anything about what he is believing, thinking or feeling, or has believed, thought or
felt, or will believe, think or feel. All I am saying is
that if this is an occasion for it, he can be expected to
believe, think or feel as a vain person does.[6] I do not
say anything about his ever having behaved in a vain
manner, but only that he is inclined to behave in such
a manner. Doubtless this would be a hazardous thing

[5] "To put it quite dogmatically, the vain man never feels vain.
Certainly, when thwarted, he feels acute dudgeon, and when un-
expectedly successful, he feels buoyant. But there is no special
thrill or pang which we call a 'feeling of vanity.' Indeed, if there
were such a recognizable specific feeling, and the vain man more
constantly experiencing it, he would be the first instead of the
last to recognize how vain he was." Ibid., p.87.
[6] "While it is true that to describe a man as vain is to say that he
is subject to a certain tendency, it is not true that the particular
exercises of this tendency consist in his registering particular thrills
or twinges. On the contrary, on hearing that a man is vain, we
expect him, in the first instance, to behave in certain ways,
namely, to talk a lot about himself, to cling to the society of the
eminent, to reject criticism, to seek the footlights and to disen-
gage himself from conversations about the merits of others. We
expect him also to indulge in roseate daydreams about his own
successes, to avoid recalling past failures, and to plan for his own
advancement. To be vain is to tend to act in these and innumerable other kindred ways." Ibid., pp.85 ff.

to say unless there was good evidence of his having behaved in a vain way, but this has to do with the *validity* of the statement, and not with the logical function. Its logical function is that of an inference-rule by
means of which we can with some probability predict
his behavior and reactions, or explain his past words
and thoughts. ("One might have expected him to act
like that, for he is a vain man.") "He is vain" is a hypothetical statement, as are all other statements describing certain traits of character, dispositions, tendencies,
motives and needs. To ascribe such things to people is
not to furnish them with so many possible causes of
possible actions, but rather to indicate the kind of
situation (for instance, an opportunity for a vain man
to advertise his merits) that will occasion certain conduct (his advertising his merits). So the statement,
"His action was prompted by vanity," is semi-hypothetical—categorical insofar as it mentions an action, but
hypothetical insofar as it is one to which the inference-
rule concerning vanity can be applied, or classified as
an action to be understood as a manifestation of vanity. Only a vain person will respond to that kind of
situation in such a way.[7]

Vanity, therefore, is not an internal phenomenon as
the Cartesian theory holds; and neither is it an ex-

[7] "To explain an act as done from a certain motive is not analogous to saying that the glass broke because a stone hit it, but to
the quite different kind of statement that the glass broke when
the stone hit it, because the glass was brittle." Ibid., pp.86 ff.

Again: "The statement 'He boasted from vanity' ought, on one
view, to be construed as saying that 'He boasted, and the cause
of his boasting was the occurrence in him of a particular feeling
or impulse of vanity.' On the other view, it is to be construed as
saying 'He boasted on meeting the stranger, and his doing so satisfies the law-like proposition that whenever he finds a chance of
securing the admiration and envy of others, he does whatever he
thinks will produce this admiration and envy.'" Ibid., p.89.

ternal phenomenon. Understood as an inference-rule, it is no more internal or external than the law of gravity. Moreover, every individual obtains knowledge about his own vanity or lack of vanity in the same way that other people obtain such knowledge, namely, by observation of behavior. I, and others, have the same access to witness my behavior and record it. Others have the same ability as I have myself to discern whether I am vain or not. I have no privileged access.

What Ryle says about the statement "His action was prompted by vanity" would be applicable to all statements which seek to explain conduct by reference to a mental concept. Statements like "He did it because he was angry" or "He did it out of cunning" are both semi-hypothetical. They report actions, but explain those actions by means of mental concepts. These are actions that can be performed only by conscious beings. If such statements are regarded as causal explanations, so that the word "because" is read like the word "because" in the statement "The apple fell because I cut its stalk," then there has been a category mistake. But if these statements are read instead as explanations or terms of a law—like "The apple fell because of the law of gravity"—the category mistake has been avoided, and the problems that emerge from such category mistakes have disappeared. Ryle is thinking here of such problems as our knowledge of other minds, the justification of our belief that other minds exist, and the traditional problems of interaction between mental and physical events.

Now, there seems to be a fundamental difference between such a statement as "He is angry" and the statement "He is conscious." The first is semi-hypothetical, explaining behavior by an inference-rule invoking the concept of anger. But could we say the same about the second statement? Surely nobody could be said to be conscious without being conscious of something. It would be nonsense to say that you are conscious, but that you are not conscious of anything; just as it would be nonsense to say that you ate but that you did not eat anything. To be conscious entails such concepts as concentration, attention, heeding, noticing, investigating, and so on. One cannot speak of consciousness without invoking some such concepts; and, likewise, if we invoke such concepts, we imply that someone is conscious.

If I do something attentively and carefully, I shall probably be right in saying that I did it well because I paid attention or exercised care. But if one takes this "because" as a causal "because," we have, according to Ryle, made a category mistake; we have made the mistake of thinking that the attention and care is the cause of what we have done attentively and carefully being done in the way it is. The so-called cause, the attention and care, is considered to be a process or act. And in this view, to do something attentively and carefully is both to perform the act of heeding (exercising attention and care), the cause, and to perform the act which is heeded, the effect; the attention and care being an internal, mental, private phenomenon and the deed itself an external, physical, public phenomenon. Now this category mistake will be avoided, according to Ryle, if we realize that we are not dealing with a case of cause and effect, but with one of explanation by reference to a law. To say that an action was done with care is to say something about the way in which it is done.[8] The criterion of whether one has

[8] "When a person hums as he walks, he is doing two things at once, either of which he might interrupt without interrupting the other. But when we speak of a person minding what he is saying, or what he is whistling, we are not saying that he is doing two things at once. He could not stop his reading while continuing his attention on it, or hand over the controls of his car while con-

read attentively or carefully is that one is able to give an account of what one has read. It is not absurd, but, indeed, quite reasonable to claim that one concentrated hard on one's reading but did not understand it. It would, however, be nonsense to say that one concentrated hard but could answer no questions at all about the reading, neither the things mentioned, nor the words used, nor even the language employed.[9] Thus the criterion of whether one has performed something attentively or carefully is not the experience of certain internal, private mental phenomena, but rather *how* one acts, behaves and reacts—how one responds, for example, to appropriate questions.

Thus, to say that one has done something carefully

---

tinuing to exercise care; though he could, of course, continue to read but cease to attend, or continue to drive but cease to take care. Since the use of such pairs of action verbs as 'read' and 'attend' or 'drive' and 'take care' may suggest that there must be two synchronous and perhaps coupled processes going on whenever both verbs are properly used, it may be helpful to remember that it is quite idiomatic to replace the heed verb with a heed adverb. We commonly speak of reading attentively, driving carefully and conning studiously, and this usage has the merit of suggesting that what is being described is one operation with a special character, and not two operations executed in different 'places' with a peculiar cable between them." Ibid., p.138.

[9] "If we want to find out whether someone has been noticing what he has been reading, we are generally content to decide the question by cross-questioning him not long afterward. If he cannot tell us anything about the gist or the wording of the chapter, if he finds no fault with other passages which contradict the original chapter, or if he expresses surprise on being informed of something already mentioned in it, then unless he has suffered concussion in the interim, or is now excited or sleepy, we are satisfied that he did not notice what he read. To notice what one reads entails being prepared to satisfy some such subsequent tests. In a similar way, certain kinds of accidents or near-accidents would satisfy us that the driver had not been taking care. To take care entails being prepared for certain sorts of emergencies." Ibid., p.139.

or attentively is to give voice to a semi-hypothetical statement, a statement that licenses inferences about the way the act was done; it is to say nothing about causes.[10] These statements predicating consciousness are also semi-hypothetical.

The statement "Man has both a body and a mind" is one that, in Wittgenstein's phrase, "bewitches our intelligence." We take it as an assertion about the existence of two entities, one internal and one external, mysteriously connected so that there is causal interaction between them. Among the illustrations Ryle uses is this one: We can say of a cricket team that it has a team spirit. If the Cartesian category mistake were made in this connection, one would fancy that the team spirit was an independently existing entity which caused the actions of the players, instead of thinking of it as something manifested in the whole conduct and behavior of the team.[11]

[10] "What distinguishes sensible from silly operations is not their parentage, but their procedure, and this holds no less for intellectual than for practical performances. . . . When I do something intelligently, i.e. thinking what I am doing, I am doing one thing and not two. My performance has a special procedure or manner, not special antecedents." Ibid., p.32.

[11] "A foreigner watching his first game of cricket learns what are the functions of the bowlers, the batsmen, the fielders, the umpires and the scorers. He then says, 'But there is no one left on the field to contribute the famous element of team spirit. I see who does the bowling, the batting and the wicket-keeping, but I do not see whose role it is to exercise *esprit de corps*.' Once more it would have to be explained that he was looking for the wrong type of thing. Team spirit is not another cricketing operation supplementary to all of the other special tasks. It is, roughly, the keenness with which each of the special tasks is performed, and performing a task keenly is not the same thing as bowling or catching, nor is it a third thing such that we can say that the bowler first bowls and then exhibits team spirit, or that a fielder at a given moment is either catching or displaying *esprit de corps*." Ibid., p.17.

What has just been said about consciousness is equally relevant to the concept of the unconscious. To explain a person's actions by means of the unconscious is not to give a causal explanation. The unconscious cannot be described by categorical, but only by hypothetical statements. To understand the unconscious is to understand what kinds of situations will prompt certain kinds of behavior, and therefore to understand why in a particular case a person acts as he does. An obvious reason for calling it the unconscious is that one is not conscious of it. I know a lot about my needs, wishes and dispositions, but I do not know all about them; and for the discovery of some of them psychiatric expertness may be needed; this is the field of the unconscious. Even so, a need or wish that is unconscious is no more a cause of action than is a conscious need or wish. It is a part of my disposition, or character. And whereas my physical appearance can be described by means of categorical statements, a description of my disposition, or character, would be not another set of categorical statements, but of hypothetical statements.

How are psychosomatic relations to be understood? There is a temptation, if not a tendency, to regard them as causal relations. Certain organic disorders are due to psychological conflicts, which the psychiatrist attempts to unveil. But here again it is important to discriminate between the categories. Confusion between causes and laws, between the categorical and the hypothetical, leads to absurdities. Neither complexes nor emotional conflicts are the *causes* of any organic disorder. To say someone suffers from a complex or emotional conflict is partly to predict which situations will prompt certain organic conditions, and partly to explain the organic conditions by showing that they are the very states to be expected in a person with such complexes in the kind of situation in which the person in question actually is.

A man in a certain emotional state will act in a certain way. His organism will likewise be in a particular condition. Just as his behavior is a manifestation (but not an effect) of his emotional state, the condition of his organism is a sign (but not an effect) of his emotional state. A person's behavior and the condition of his organism are logically different. His behavior is a *display* or manifestation of a particular emotional state, whereas the organic condition is a *sign* of it. The fact that I run away is a manifestation of my fear, whereas the rapid beating of my heart is only a sign of it. It would be absurd for me to say that I always run away from alarming situations, but I am never afraid; but it would not be absurd to maintain that whenever I am afraid I run away, but that somehow my heart doesn't beat any faster. Yet both the fact that I am running away and the fact that my heart is beating faster have, in a relevant context, a common cause—the alarming situation. The rapid beating of the heart does not make me afraid nor make me run; the heart beats fast and I run because I am afraid. Although I can explain my behavior and certain organic conditions by fear, it is a category mistake to classify that fear as a cause. It can no more be a cause, or an effect, than the law of gravity can be a cause or an effect.

The Concept of Mind is a substantial book, which analyzes many problems in considerable detail. Naturally, it is impossible to do justice to it in a short sketch. It is a work that must be studied at first hand. I have attempted to do no more here than indicate the logical framework of its argument, and to outline the category mistake on which Ryle believes that the Cartesian theory rests.

2

Ryle's attitude in *The Concept of Mind* to the Cartesian theory is frankly polemical—polemical in the sense that he attacks it as the fruit of a misunderstanding of the logic of language. Peter Strawson's paper, "On Referring,"[12] is no less polemical; he too is attacking what he believes to be a mistaken conception of meaning. Strawson's paper is Wittgensteinian in the sense that it argues that the meaning of a sentence is not what it refers to, but the rules for its correct use. His polemic is directed chiefly against Russell. In his celebrated and historic paper "On Denoting,"[13] Russell says: "By the law of the excluded middle, either 'A is B' or 'A is not B' must be true. Hence either 'The present king of France is bald' or 'The present king of France is not bald' must be true. Yet if we enumerated the men who are bald and then the men who are not bald, we should not find the present king of France in either list. Hegelians, who love a synthesis, will probably conclude that he wears a wig."[14] Russell's own analysis of the sentence "The present king of France is bald" is that the sentence has meaning but is false. Now, on what grounds is it false? Clearly not on the grounds that the present king of France is not bald. It is false simply because no present king of France exists. In other words, what is false in the sentence is "The present king of France exists," or, in more Russellian terms, "One and only one person exists such that this person is at present king of France." This existential

[12] *Mind*, 1950. Reprinted in (and here quoted from) *Essays in Conceptual Analysis*, ed. Antony Flew, 1956.
[13] *Mind*, 1905. Reprinted in (and here quoted from) Russell's *Logic and Language*, ed. by Robert C. Marsh, 1956.
[14] Ibid., pp.526 ff.

proposition is part of what is stated by the proposition "The present king of France is bald." Thus the latter can be false for two different reasons: either because no present king of France exists, or because the present king of France is not bald. If, instead, we take the proposition "The present king of France is not bald," then, according to Russell, it can be both true and false. It is false because it states that a present (non-bald) king of France exists. It is false because it states something that is not the case. But it is true if it states that there is no present king of France. If the sentence "The present king of France is not bald" is false (intended as an assertion of the existence of a present king of France), then the expression has what Russell calls a "primary occurrence." But if the sentence is true (i.e. intended as an assertion of the nonexistence of a present king of France), then the expression has a "secondary occurrence."[15]

It follows that in Russell's view, "The present king of France is bald" is significant but false. To be significant, a statement must have a truth-value, be either true or false. Therefore, according to Russell, every assertion must be true or false or meaningless. "The present king of France is bald" is a meaningful sentence (though false) in that it is existential. The existential assertion is part of what is maintained. And the existential statement is not a statement with a logical subject about which something can be predicated, but a sentence without a logical subject.

The existential assertion is part of the sentence "The present king of France is bald," for if it was not, then the sentence would be meaningless, and therefore not false. It would be meaningless because it would function as a logical subject, i.e. as a name or expression

[15] Ibid., pp.52 ff.

denoting a person; and for a name or denoting expression to be meaningful, something must exist for it to name or denote.[16]

What Strawson rejects is Russell's claim that every sentence must be true or false or meaningless. He rejects at the same time Russell's claim that a sentence can be significant only if what is named, or denoted by the logical subject, exists. Strawson's case is built on a distinction between a sentence (or an expression) and the use of a sentence in a statement. Strawson gives as an example the sentence "The king of France is wise." The sentence is meaningful, but is it true or false? In itself it is neither one nor the other. The sentence itself has no truth-value; but the use of it has a truth-value, and that truth-value depends on the situation. Suppose a person uttered the sentence (i.e. used it to make an assertion) during the reign of Louis XIV, and another used it during the reign of Louis XV. In the first case, it might be held to be a true assertion; in the second, it might be held to be a false assertion.

Hence it is a misunderstanding to ask whether the sentence itself is true or false. It is only when a sentence is used to make an assertion[17] that one can ask whether it is true or false. On the other hand, while a sentence as such can be neither true nor false, it can be either meaningful or meaningless. As a sentence, "The king of France is wise" is neither true nor false, but meaningful. A sentence is meaningful if there are rules for its use as an assertion.[18]

[16] See Strawson, op. cit., pp.24 ff.
[17] A sentence can, of course, be used for various other purposes besides making assertions. But Strawson, in this paper, is concerned with this use only.
[18] "To give the meaning of a sentence is to give general directions for its use in making true or false assertions. It is not to

It is also necessary to distinguish between an expression and the use of an expression. The expression "The king of France" in the sentence "The king of France is wise" is not one that names or refers to somebody. It is only when it is used in an assertion that the expression names or refers to somebody. And that use determines to whom it refers. If the expression "The king of France" is used during the reign of Louis XIV, it will refer to Louis XIV, and if it is used during the reign of Louis XV, it will refer to Louis XV.

Sentences are not about things or persons; but the same sentence can be used to state something about different things and persons. An expression neither names nor refers to things and persons, but one and the same expression can be used to name or refer to different things and persons. But in spite of all this, an expression can still have a meaning. It has meaning if there are rules for using it to refer to or state anything at all.[19]

Thus meaning and truth belong to two distinct logical categories: meaning is a function of sentences and expressions, whereas truth or falsity and referring and mentioning are functions of the use of sentences and expressions.[20] Meaning belongs to sentences and ex-

talk about any particular occasion of the use of the sentence. . . . The meaning of a sentence cannot be identified with the assertion it is used, on a particular occasion, to make." Strawson, op. cit., p.30.

[19] "To give the meaning of an expression (in the sense in which I am using the word) is to give *general directions* for its use to refer to or mention particular objects or persons. . . . The meaning of an expression cannot be identified with the object it is used, on a particular occasion, to refer to." Ibid., p.30.

[20] "Meaning (in at least one important sense) is a function of the sentence or expression; mentioning and referring and truth or falsity are functions of the use of the sentence or expression. . . . For to talk about the meaning of an expression or sentence is not to talk about its use on a particular occasion, but about the

pressions; truth-values and referring belong to the use of sentences and expressions.

The sentence "The king of France is wise" is thus not a sentence *about* somebody or something, for sentences are not statements. It is only when a sentence *is used* that it becomes a statement about the king of France. According to Strawson, Russell is guilty of the mistake of thinking (1) that "The king of France is wise" is a false sentence; and (2) that "The king of France is wise" is an existential sentence. Strawson holds that the expression "The king of France" is a referring expression which specifies a set of predicates that either can or cannot be predicated about somebody or something.

Russell's belief (1) that "The king of France is wise" is a false sentence is mistaken because sentences are not true or false but only meaningful or meaningless. Russell's belief (2) that "The king of France is wise" is an existential statement is mistaken because it is based on the erroneous assumption that the sentence is false, from which Russell goes on to argue that since the falsity cannot rest on the ground that the king of France is not wise, then it must rest on the ground that the king of France does not exist. Moreover, as Russell believes he has shown that an existential statement has no logical subject, it follows that the expression "The king of France" cannot be a logical subject, i.e. it cannot be an expression that names, denotes or refers to somebody. According to Strawson's view that

---

rules, habits and conventions governing its correct use on all occasions, to refer or to assert. So the question of whether a sentence or expression is significant or not has nothing whatever to do with the question whether the sentence, uttered on a particular occasion, is, on that occasion, being used to make a true-or-false assertion or not, or of whether the expression is, on that occasion, being used to refer to, or mention, anything at all." Ibid., pp.30 ff.

only the use of the sentence (and not the sentence itself) can be true or false, then "The king of France is wise" can be false only if the king of France is not wise, and not false (and this is a crucial point in Strawson's analysis) on the grounds that the king of France does not exist.

This point may be elaborated a little. Suppose that on August 1, 1964, somebody maintained (used the sentence): "France is a monarchy." This would be a false assertion. A sufficient answer would be, "No, it is not." The assertion "France is not a monarchy" would be an assertion contradicting the first. To maintain both would be plainly illogical. Now suppose someone on the same date said, "The king of France is wise." This is not a false assertion. It would be misleading to answer, "No, he is not." To ask whether it is true or false is not an adequate question; if a person were really serious in saying such a thing, it would be difficult to know how to answer.[21] The statement "The king of France is wise" is one which implies that there is a king of France, implies, in the sense that if there is no king of France it is not a genuine use of the sentence "The king of France is wise," but is what Strawson terms a secondary use.[22]

The assertion "The king of France is wise" implies (in this sense of "implies") that there is a king of France. But this does not imply (as Russell assumed) that the assertion "The king of France exists" is part of the assertion "The king of France is wise," so that a denial of this existential sentence would be a contra-

[21] "You might, if he were obviously serious (had a dazed, astray-in-the-centuries look), say something like, 'I'm afraid you must be under a misapprehension. France is not a monarchy. There is no king of France.'" Ibid., p.34.
[22] In his original article in *Mind*, Strawson called it a "spurious" or "pseudo-use." In the reprint, he mentions in a footnote (p.35) that he now prefers to speak of "secondary use."

diction of the sentence "The king of France is wise."
To reply to someone who says the king of France is
wise that there is no king of France, is not, according
to Strawson, to contradict him. The reply is a matter
of showing that the question of its truth or falsity does
not arise.[23]

A "secondary" use of a meaningful sentence does not
result in a meaningless statement, it is simply the use
of a meaningful sentence that does not result in a true
or false statement.[24] Thus Strawson's criticism of Russell is directed against Russell's failure to distinguish
between a sentence and its use, and his belief that the
meaning of an expression is what it refers to. Strawson
does not examine, or criticize, Russell's analysis of the
existential statement "The king of France exists."
Strawson does, however, establish that Russell has con-
fused the sentence and the use of the sentence. The
sentence "The king of France exists" is significant but
neither true nor false, and it refers to no one. Its meaning is not what it refers to, but the rules governing its

[23] "To say 'The king of France is wise' is, in some sense of 'imply,' to imply that there is a king of France. But this is a very
special and odd sense of 'imply.' 'Implies' in this sense is certainly not equivalent to 'entails' (or 'logically implies'). And this
comes from the fact that when, in response to his statement, we
say (as we should) 'There is no king of France,' we should certainly not say we are contradicting the statement that the king
of France is wise. We are certainly not saying that it is false. We
are, rather, giving a reason for saying that the question of whether
it is true or false simply does not arise." Strawson, op. cit., p.34.
[24] "The sentence 'The king of France is wise' is certainly significant; but this does not mean that any particular use of it is
true or false. . . . So when we utter the sentence without in fact
mentioning anybody by the use of the phrase 'The king of
France,' the sentence does not cease to be significant: we simply
fail to mention anybody by this particular use of that perfectly
significant phrase. . . . It is, if you like, a spurious use of the sentence, and a spurious use of the expression; though we may (or
may not) mistakenly think it a genuine use." Ibid., pp.34 ff.

use. Moreover, the sentence is not, except in a merely grammatical way, a subject-predicate sentence. It does not predicate anything about somebody. If the sentence is used, it is correct, as Russell maintains, but it has no logical subject.[25]

It is worth mentioning here that before Strawson's paper, "On Referring," was published, there appeared in *Analysis* (1950) a paper by Peter Geach entitled "Russell's Theory of Descriptions," which touched on the same problems. Without employing Strawson's distinction between a sentence and its use, and without attacking Russell's belief that meaning is denoting, Geach criticizes Russell's analysis of the sentence "The king of France is bald." Geach argues that to maintain, as Russell does, that this sentence is false is to be guilty of what he calls "the fallacy of many questions." What Geach has in mind is this: suppose somebody is asked if he is happier since his wife's death. In order for a man to be able to answer this question with a yes or no, two other questions must already have been answered affirmatively, namely, whether he has been married and whether his wife is dead.[26] If the answers to these questions are negative, the answer to the original question is neither yes nor no, because that question cannot be asked at all. And if such a question is seriously put to a man, unmarried or with a loving wife, then the man who is asked it does not say yes or no, he gives only reasons why it cannot be asked.[27]

[25] It would require considerable imagination to think of a situation in which anybody would say, "The king of France exists." Perhaps during the French Revolution, but before January 21, 1793, a French Royalist might proclaim, "The king of France exists!"

[26] *Analysis* (1950), p.33.

[27] "When a question does not arise, the only proper way of answering it is to say so, and explain the reason: the 'plain' affirmative or negative answer, though grammatically and logically

To ask whether the present king of France is bald involves, among others, the question whether somebody is at present on the throne of France. If this latter question is not answered affirmatively, then the question about baldness cannot be asked. Hence an affirmative to the question is not a false answer, it is what Geach calls "out of place."[28]

Geach accepts Russell's analysis of existential sentences,[29] but argues that his analysis of such sentences as "The king of France is bald" is wrong; for such sentences are not themselves existential, and can be stated only if other existential sentences are true. Thus Geach and Strawson agree in some part of their criticism of Russell.

3

We have already spoken of Wittgenstein's belief that philosophers commonly misunderstand the logic of language or the logical characteristic of particular language-games. We have also mentioned what Austin calls the "descriptive fallacy," the error of taking as descriptive sentences that have those functions which are not descriptive, and so giving rise to philosophical problems. In a celebrated essay entitled "The Ascription of Responsibility and Rights," Professor H. L. A. Hart ap-

---

possible, is out of place. This does not go against the laws of contradiction and excluded middle; what these laws tell us is that if the question arose, 'Yes' and 'No' would be exclusive alternatives." Ibid., p.33.

[28] Geach adds: "This view agrees, I think, with common sense; a plain man, if pressed for an answer, would be very likely to reply 'Don't be silly; there isn't a king of France.'" Ibid., p. 34.

[29] "Russell's analysis of ordinary existential assertions containing definite descriptions, like 'The king of France exists' is quite adequate." Ibid., p.34.

plies the same technique to problems that occur in the fields of morals and jurisprudence.[30]

Hart examines certain legal concepts, that is to say, those used in law courts and employed in legal arguments. All these, Hart says, have a certain logical characteristic in common, they are what he terms "defeasible."[31] He explains what he means in this way: when someone is accused of something, concepts like "murder," "fraud," "breach of contract" are invoked. Now, according to Hart, to validate an accusation is to be able to reject, refute any attempt to defeat the accusation. In other words, the proof is not positive, but negative. This procedure does not begin with a definition of the particular concepts followed by an investigation of different actions to see if they come within the terms of these definitions. Such a procedure would be positive. In fact, the meanings of the various legal concepts are not determined by definition, for no particular set of conditions both sufficient and necessary exists. The procedure followed in determining the validity of an accusation is, paradoxically, one of showing the impossibility of establishing the invalidity of accusation. An accusation stands until it has been defeated.

There are two ways in which an accusation can be challenged. Suppose that John Smith has been accused of murdering his wife by putting arsenic in her coffee. The accusation is valid *unless* (1) it can be established that he did not put arsenic in his wife's coffee, or (2) it can be shown that although he did put arsenic in her coffee, special circumstances prevail, so that it cannot

[30] In the *Proceedings of the Aristotelian Society* (1948–49). Reprinted in, and here quoted from, *Logic and Language*, First Series, ed. by A. G. N. Flew. Hart (b.1907) is Professor of Jurisprudence at Oxford, and a leading authority on the philosophy of law. He is the author of *The Concept of Law, Law, Liberty and Morality*, etc.

[31] Hart, op. cit., p.148.

be considered a case of murder. Perhaps it can be shown that John Smith thought it was sugar, or some medicine ordered by her doctor. Defeating the accusation consists either in a denial of the facts on which the case is based or in the establishment of special circumstances that lead to the accusation being dropped.[32]

The concepts concerned can thus be neither defined nor be adequately characterized, for a definition of the concept would have to include every single circumstance that would invalidate it, which would be impossible.[33] Now, the belief has prevailed (says Hart) that it is possible to give a complete definition of such concepts, or, in other words, to state the sufficient and necessary conditions for the uses of the concept. It has been assumed, for example, that such definition could be provided for the concepts used in demanding that an action be done with foresight of its consequences and be done voluntarily. The inclusion of these demands encourages the belief that we are dealing with *positive* factors, namely, the psychological state of foresight and voluntariness, and the belief that the validity of an accusation has been established if, at the time of

---

[32] "For the accusations or claims upon which law courts adjudicate can usually be challenged or opposed in two ways. First, by a denial of the facts on which they are based (technically called a traverse or joinder of issue), and secondly by something quite different, namely, a plea that although all the circumstances on which a claim could succeed are present, yet in the particular case, the claim or accusation should not succeed because other circumstances are present which bring the case under some recognized head of exception, the effect of which is either to defeat the claim or accusation altogether, or to 'reduce' it so that only a weaker claim can be sustained. Thus a plea of 'provocation' in murder cases, if successful, 'reduces' what would otherwise be murder to manslaughter." Ibid., pp.147 ff.

[33] "The concept is irreducibly defensible in character, and to ignore this is to misrepresent it." Ibid., p.150.

the deed, the presence of such psychological states in the accused person can be proved. Now such thinking, according to Hart, is mistaken. Such concepts as "foresight" and "voluntariness" are *defeasible*. There are no such sufficient and necessary conditions that, if satisfied, would provide proof of foresight and voluntariness. In each particular case foresight and voluntariness is established by proving that the concepts of "ignorance" and "coercion" *cannot* be applied. To say that an action is voluntary is not to ascribe a particular property (the property of voluntariness) to it; rather it is to deny that certain other properties can be applied— properties such as physical compulsion, coercion by threats, accident, mistakes of fact, and so forth. In other words, by calling a concept defeasible one says that the concept has no positive characteristics, and that it can be used only by virtue of the fact that no negative characteristics exist.[34]

Whether a defeasible concept is applicable in a particular case is a matter for argument; but the conclusion of such an argument is not a conclusion in the sense that is known in deductive or inductive logic. The conclusion is a *judgment*, based on the weighing of the arguments and cases presented. If, for instance, the judgment or decision concerns the existence or nonexistence of a contract, and thus whether the accused party has committed a breach of contract, the adjudicating court must decide whether the arguments of the defense have been forceful enough to establish that no contract exists. If they do not succeed, the decision will be that a contract *does* exist. The sentence "A contract exists" is not used as a conclusion reached analytically or empirically. Nor is it a description or a report. It is a

[34] Hart notes (Ibid., p.153) that Aristotle treats the concept of "voluntary" as a defeasible concept. (*Nicomachean Ethics*, Book III)

decision or judgment, and, as such, more or less wise, sound or bad, perhaps even right or wrong, but neither true nor false.[35]

Consider the sentences: (1) This is mine, and (2) This is yours. These can be used descriptively. If I point to a coat in a cloakroom and say, "This is mine," I am using the sentence descriptively. But the sentence has other uses that are nondescriptive. If I am in a situation where I have a right to choose something, I can choose by pointing at a thing and saying, "This is mine." Or I can give something to somebody with the words, "This is yours." In such cases the use of the sentence is not descriptive but *performatory*.

The term "performatory" as a means of classifying utterances was introduced by the late Professor John L. Austin. As examples of performatory utterances Austin suggested "I swear" and "I promise." A person who swears, who utters the words "I swear" in the appropriate situation, does not, with these words, describe or report something he has done; uttering the words is itself the better part of the action, or ritual, of swearing. Only in a very complicated situation could the sentence be used descriptively—for example, if a person taking an oath was asked what he was doing, he might answer, "I am swearing." But the general and normal use of the sentence is the performatory use.[36]

[35] "Since the judge is literally deciding that, on the facts before him, a contract does or does not exist, and to do this is neither to describe the facts nor to make inductive or deductive inferences from the statement of facts, what he does may be either a right or a wrong decision, or a good or bad judgment, and can be either affirmed or reversed and (when he has no jurisdiction to decide the question) may be quashed or discharged. What cannot be said of it is that it is either true or false, logically necessary or absurd." Hart, op. cit., p.155.

[36] For Austin's own account of "performatory utterances" see his paper, "Other Minds," reprinted in *Logic and Language*, Second

Besides their descriptive and performatory uses, sentences such as "This is mine" and "This is yours" may also be employed in connection with a defeasible concept. If I recognize a person's rights or ascribe a right to him, I may do so because I believe that this or that is rightly his. I see a watch fall from a man's pocket, and pick it up and hand it to him with the words: "This is yours." A few moments later I see the man being arrested and accused of stealing the watch. Now, the sentence "This is yours" was not used as a description, although the sentence "This watch fell from your pocket" would have been a descriptive statement, and would still remain true, despite his being arrested for theft. The sentence "This is yours" is no longer valid. I am not willing to confirm it. It has been defeated. That is to say, the sentence includes a defeasible concept. What it does is not to describe, but to *ascribe*. And ascriptive statements are defeasible.[37]

Next, let us consider sentences of another kind. Compare "It was Peter who threw the stone" with "Peter is throwing the stone." The second will generally be used descriptively, but the first is not normally used descriptively. Sentences like "Peter did it," "You did it," "I did it" are used to accuse, to ascribe responsibility and to confess; and all these utterances differ from describing or reporting. Again, compare (A) He beat her, with (B) His right arm moved with great force and finally struck her left cheek. The latter is (generally) descriptive; the former is (generally) non-descriptive. To say, "He beat her," is not to report the movements of his arm, but rather to indict and ascribe

Series, pp.143 ff. Strawson also used the term "performatory," and suggests that certain uses of the expression "It is true" are of this kind. See his essay, "Truth," in *Analysis IX*, reprinted in *Philosophy and Analysis*, ed. by M. Macdonald, pp.272 ff.

[37] The word "ascriptive" is Hart's; he opposes it to "descriptive."

responsibility. The sentence "He beat her" is not a conclusion from an empirical premise. Sentence (A) and sentence (B) belong to two different categories. If sentence (A) were a logical conclusion from sentence (B), it could not be the case that the descriptive sentence (B) was true and the sentence (A) "He beat her" false. In reality, however, this could well be the case. It is conceivable that his arm moved as described but that he did not *beat* her; the movement may have been accidental or convulsive. In other words, the sentence "He beat her" is defeasible. If it stands as it is, this shows that it has proved impossible to argue convincingly that the action was done inadvertently or by mistake. If it cannot be defeated, that is, it holds good. And whether it can be defeated or not is something to be judged or decided; not settled by deduction or induction.

The conclusion that legal concepts of this kind are defeasible undermines the widely held philosophical theory that the meaning of a proposition lies in its truth-condition. For a sentence involving a defeasible concept is valid if and only if none of the numerous and heterogeneous statements that could refute it are true.[38]

This is indeed a fatal argument against the theory

[38] "Consideration of the defeasible character of legal concepts . . . shows how wrong it would be to succumb to the temptation, offered by modern theories of meaning, to identify the meaning of a legal concept, say 'contract,' with the statement of the conditions in which contracts are held to exist; since owing to the defeasible character of the concept, such a statement, though it would express the necessary and sometimes sufficient conditions for the application of 'contract,' could not express conditions which were always sufficient. But, of course, any such theory of the meaning of legal concepts would fail for far more fundamental reasons, for it could not convey the composite character of these concepts nor allow for the distinctive features due to the fact that the elements in the compound are of distinct logical types." Hart, op. cit., pp.154 ff.

of truth as verification (just as Strawson's is a fatal argument). For to maintain that sentences such as "It was Peter who did it" or "He beat her" are meaningless would be absurd, yet such would seem to be entailed by the verification theory in the light of Hart's analysis.

4

The use of such sentences as "It is yellow," "It is square," or "It is an inch long" is descriptive. Their function is unambiguous, and cannot cause misunderstanding. But just as often—perhaps more often—we use sentences of a totally different type, sentences where the predicates are not empirical, like "yellow" and "square," but evaluative—words like "good," "bad," "first-rate," "mediocre," and so on. Many philosophers have tended to classify these words as descriptive—to put them into the one class of sentences they have been willing to regard as meaningful. However, as we have seen, a classification of sentences as either significant or meaningless is not an exhaustive classification. Many, perhaps most sentences fall into neither class. Now, this has particular relevance to evaluative, or grading sentences. They are not meaningless, nor is their function descriptive.

In a paper entitled "On Grading,"[39] the Oxford philosopher J. O. Urmson[40] studies the use of sentences that function as evaluations. He works from the simple and homely example of grading apples. Now, let us imagine that there are only two "grading labels" for apples, good and bad. Whether an apple is to be graded

[39] *Mind*, 1950. Reprinted in, and here quoted from, *Logic and Language*, Second Series.
[40] (b.1915) Fellow of Corpus Christi College, sometime Professor of Philosophy at St. Andrew's. Author of *Philosophical Analysis*, etc.

good or bad depends on various empirical properties of the apple concerned. To be good it must be of a certain size and ripeness, free from blemishes, not misshapen, and so forth. Descriptions of the apple framed in such language are the criteria for the use of the sentence "This apple is good."

Apples, of course, are not the only things that are graded. Qualities of a different nature are demanded if a book, a car, or a summer holiday is to be called good. The criteria for judging one thing good are A, B, and C; for another, D, E, and F; for a third, G, H, and I—and so on. Now, this seems to open two possibilities. Either it can be held that what the word "good" means is the criteria for its use, and hence the word "good" has countless meanings; or it can be held that the word "good" has only one meaning, and hence its meaning is not identical with the criteria for a thing being called good.

If we confine ourselves to a single case, say the one where the criteria for being graded "good" are A, B, and C, we find that if one identifies the meaning of the word "good" with the criteria for its use, the meaning of the word "good" is identical with A, B, and C. In other words, the sentence "This is good" becomes an empirical statement which means the same as "This is A, B, and C." The word "good" becomes a shorthand way of saying "This is A, B, and C."[41] Urmson holds this view, known in ethics as naturalism, to be mistaken. One of his arguments against it is this: suppose that the grading of apples is done by putting the good apples (those with qualities A, B, and C) into one box and putting the bad apples (those lacking the qualities A, B, and C) into another. Next, imagine that someone who has never tasted an apple and doesn't know that

41 Urmson, op. cit., p.169 and pp.175 ff.

an apple can be liked or disliked is employed to help
put the apples with the qualities A, B, and C in the box
marked GOOD and the other apples in the box marked
BAD. He has no other knowledge of what he is doing
than the knowledge that certain empirical characteristics determine whether an apple is put in one box or
another. Can he be said to grade? Of course not, for in
a certain sense he has no idea what he is doing. He
may, for instance, believe that it is a game, or perhaps
a nongrading classification or something similar.[42] But
if the word "good" meant no more than the conjunc-
tion of the empirical properties A, B, and C, then he
would be grading just as much as one who knew what
he was doing and why.[43]

Another of Urmson's arguments is this: If the sentence "This is good" means the same as the sentence
"This is A, B, and C" then, as we have seen, the word
"good" will have countless meanings. For it is only in
one particular case that the criteria for "good" are A,
B, and C; in another case, they will be D, E, and F, and
so on. And as we grade countless different things, so
are there countless different criteria for the use of the
word "good." Urmson believes, however, that the word
"good" has only one meaning, and he thinks this for the
following reason. I understand the statement "This is

---

[42] "Without further information, our intelligent apprentice, although he would have learned to grade the apples, or sleepers, in
the sense in which a parrot can learn to speak English, might
realize no more than the parrot that he was grading. He might
not guess but that he was playing some rather tedious game, or
tidying up, just as if he were sorting out white and black draughts
pieces, or assisting in some scientific classification; he need not
speculate on what he is doing at all. As we might say that the
parrot was not really speaking English, knowing just what we
meant to convey by this, so we might say that the apprentice, unlike you, was not really grading." Ibid., pp.160 ff.
[43] Ibid., p.178.

a good horse" whether I know anything about horses or not. I don't need to know what the criteria are to understand the statement. I cannot justify it, but I can understand it. But if the meaning of the statement were its truth-conditions, then I should not be able to understand it, as I do. I understand it because I know that the word "good" is used as a grading label, and this understanding is quite independent of any understanding of the reasons why a particular thing is graded "good."[44]

However, Urmson does not pass from the belief that "good" is not the same as the empirical properties[45] A, B, and C to the conclusion (favored by ethical intuitionists) that "good" is an independent, nonnaturalistic quality. For to think this would again be to misunderstand the function that the word "good" performs. The word "good" is not the name of a naturalistic or a nonnaturalistic quality, for the simple reason that it is not a name at all.

To use the sentence "This is good" is to grade. And to grade is neither to name nor to describe nor to do anything other than simply grading.[46] Grading is the activity of placing a thing in a class which ranks above or below other classes. To say that one class is above another is to say that because of certain criteria (presupposed if not mentioned) it is more commendable.

Urmson compares the distinction between grading

[44] Ibid., p.178.
[45] Urmson's arguments directed against ethical naturalism demonstrate that the so-called "naturalistic fallacy" really is a fallacy.
[46] "At some stage we must say firmly (why not now?) that to describe is to describe, to grade is to grade, and to express one's feelings is to express one's feelings, and that none of these is reducible to either of the others; nor can any of them be reduced to, be defined in terms of, anything else. We can merely bring out similarities and differences by examples and comparisons." Urmson, op. cit., p.171.

and the grading criteria to the distinction between having a legal right and the legal qualifications for having a right. Nobody would say that "I am legally of age" is the same as "I am 21 years old or more." Again, take the case of an official dealing with applications for grants. The ministry lays down certain conditions which must be satisfied if the official is to approve of the application. Now, the official may sometimes write "Approved" on the application form. This word "Approved" is not identical with "The application fulfills all the conditions for approval." That it is not identical may be seen from the fact that it would be a contradiction to write after "Approved" "But not approved," while it would not be a contradiction to write, "The application fulfills all the conditions for approval—But not approved." Admittedly this latter would be a surprising endorsement and would require some explanation; but it would not be a self-contradictory endorsement.

Now, the sentence "This is good" may in some respects, but not all, be compared with sentences like "I approve,"[47] or "I recommend." Generally these sentences are used only when certain criteria are satisfied. The criteria are neither named nor described, but presupposed. These criteria are what would justify the approval or the recommendation. To say, "I approve," or, "I recommend," is not to describe something I am doing. It is to *do* something, namely, to approve or recommend. This applies equally to saying, "This is good." To utter the words is to grade and commend; and this utterance will be justified if certain criteria—different criteria in different cases—are satisfied; but, again, the actual criteria are presupposed, not stated. In every case the use of the sentence "This is good" is to be substantiated or justified by criteria.

[47] Ibid., pp.173 ff.

To grade is not to express something subjective, Urmson maintains, but, on the contrary, to express something objective. Of course, I may sometimes say of a thing, "This is good," and mean no more than that I like it, but if I know that it is an assertion not well substantiated, I am unlikely to make it in front of an expert.[48] Generally accepted criteria for the grading of different things do exist. There are wine experts, art experts, and many other kinds of experts, each mastering his respective criteria. Their grading does not merely represent their own tastes, but is a use of criteria, the knowledge of which is their speciality. Thus it is no logical absurdity to say that a thing is good but that personally one does not like it.[49]

When sentences like "This is good" are used, generally established criteria are necessary presuppositions, but no such presuppositions are required when one is merely giving voice to personal likes and dislikes. The sentence "I like it" belongs to a different logical category than "This is good." The former is subjective, the latter objective. To the first one may add, without con-

---

[48] "Grading statements being, as I maintain, objectively decidable, they are, for many reasons, more important and impressive than mere indications of personal likes and dislikes. We therefore tend to use them when all we are entitled to do is to express our likes and dislikes. Thus, I might easily say, 'That's a good horse,' being ignorant of the criteria for a good horse and therefore really only entitled to say that I like the look of it. We really know this, as becomes clear when we reflect that only a very conceited person would chance his arm by saying, 'That's a good horse,' unless he knew or believed that his companion was as ignorant of horses as he was. We might say it to a city clerk—but not to a Newmarket trainer." Ibid., p.178.

[49] "Thus, even if one happens to hate all cheese, one will still be able sensibly to distinguish good from bad cheese; *mutatis mutandis* the same applies to lapdogs or anything else." Ibid., p.180.

tradition, "but it is not good"; but to add these words to the second is to utter a clear contradiction.

The logical structure of the sentence "This is good" is quite distinct from any question about the validity or relevance of any criterion that may be invoked in support of it. It remains a sentence presupposing generally established criteria whether those criteria are, for example, utilitarian or intuitionist. Besides, it is hardly possible to give a general answer to a general question about why we have the criteria we do have. A concrete question can be given a concrete answer, however trivial or commonplace. The question why a knife must be sharp to be good is just as trivial as the question why a doctor must have both knowledge and experience to be a good doctor. On the other hand, the question why a work of art with such and such qualities is good is by no means trivial. However, to enter on such problems would take us beyond the subject of Urmson's paper and also beyond the limits of this essay.

AFTERWORD

As already mentioned in the preface, since this book was originally published, several of Wittgenstein's *Nachegelassenen Schriften* have become available, and innumerable works on Wittgenstein have appeared. It may be useful to add a few words on some recent Wittgenstein research, particularly where such research and studies disagree with points made on the previous pages.

I stated earlier in this study that no unbroken line leads from the *Tractatus* to the *Philosophical Investigations*; there is no logical sequence between the two books, but rather a logical gap. The thought of the later work is a negation of the thought of the earlier. In his book *Wittgenstein's Conception of Philosophy* (1969) K. T. Fann maintains that I am radically mistaken. Although Wittgenstein in the *Philosophical Investigations* criticizes his own views in the *Tractatus,* he nevertheless says that the *Tractatus* was not all wrong. According to Fann there is an important continuity between the two works due to the fact that in both books Wittgenstein conceives of philosophical problems as arising from our misunderstanding of the logic of language, and to the fact that philosophy is not a science but an activity of elucidation and classification.

The view that there are an earlier and a later Wittgenstein is also criticized by Peter Winch. In his introduction to *Studies in the Philosophy of Wittgenstein* (1969) he terms the view "disastrously mistaken." The alleged unity of Wittgenstein's philosophy he finds in the fact that in both works Wittgenstein deals with problems about the nature of logic, about the relation of logic to language, and about the application of logic in language to reality.

In a recently published study, *The Legacy of Wittgenstein* (1982) Anthony Kenny writes, "Like my earlier book, this collection of essays is devoted to stressing the continuity of Wittgenstein's philosophy and of his conception of the nature of philosophy." The earlier book he mentions has the title *Wittgenstein* and was published in 1973. The last chapter of that book he calls "The Continuity of Wittgenstein's Philosophy." He then admits that the view (which after all is a basic assumption in the *Tractatus*) that the ultimate elements of language are names that designate simple objects and that, consequently, elementary propositions are concatenations of these names, each such proposition being independent of every other such proposition, is a mistaken view. Nevertheless, Kenny maintains that Wittgenstein upheld some sort of modified picture theory. I shall not argue against it; it should be emphasized, however, that the kind of picture theory basic to the *Tractatus* Wittgenstein denied in the *Philosophical Investigations.*

G. H. von Wright, one of the few who were intimately acquainted with Wittgenstein, writes in *Wittgenstein* (1982):

> "It will probably remain a matter of future debate to what extent there is continuity between the 'early' Wittgenstein of the *Tractatus* and the 'later' Wittgenstein of the *Investigations.* The writings from 1929 to 1932 testify to a continuous development and struggle—out of the former work in the

144

direction of the later. The Blue Book of 1933–34 conveys more the impression of a first, still somewhat rough verison of a radically new philosophy. I myself find it difficult to fit the Blue Book into the development of Wittgenstein's thoughts. The Brown Book is a somewhat different case. It may be regarded as a preliminary version of the beginning of the *Investigations*" (p. 27).

A few lines later von Wright includes here almost verbatim, what he also wrote in his *Biographical Sketch*: "The young Wittgenstein had learned from Frege and Russell. His problems were in part theirs. The later Wittgenstein, in my view, has no ancestors in the history of thought. His work signals a radical departure from previously existing paths of philosophy."

Von Wright then adds the following note:

"I have seen this statement, and the one preceding it, contested. But I think they are substantially correct and also important. The *Tractatus* belongs in a definite tradition in European philosophy, extending back beyond Frege and Russell at least to Leibniz. Wittgenstein's so-called 'later philosophy,' as I see it, is quite different. Its *spirit* is unlike anything I know in Western thought and in many ways opposed to aims and methods in traditional philosophy. This is not incompatible with the fact—about which more is known now than when this essay was first published—that many of Wittgenstein's later ideas have seeds in works which he had read and conversations he had with others."

It is interesting to note what Wittgenstein himself says about this in *Vermischte Bemerkungen* (edited by G. H. von Wright and translated into English by Peter Winch as *Culture and Value*, Basil Blackwell, Oxford, 1980), especially pp. 18 ff. and p. 36. In the latter place he says: "I believe that my originality (if that is the right word) is an originality belonging to the soil rather than to the seed. (Perhaps I have no seed of my own). Sow a seed in my soil and it will grow differently than it would in any other soil." Wittgenstein's remark to von Wright quoted both in von Wright's *Biographical Sketch* and in his book *Wittgenstein* (respectively p. 16 and p. 28), that discussion with Sraffa made him feel like a tree from which all branches had been cut, surely indicates that Wittgenstein himself thought there was a logical gap between the *Tractatus* and his later philosophy.

This is not the place to enter into a lengthy discussion about the problem. Personally I cannot see any reason to change what, on this topic, I have originally said in this book. The essential point is, I think, that since Wittgenstein, according to his own admittance, found that it did not make sense to say that a fact has a logical form— i.e. the foundation on which the *Tractatus'* picture theory rests—the picture theory had to be abandoned. In a fundamental sense the concept of a picture theory is rejected in Wittgenstein's later philosophy.

Another problem discussed in the post-Wittgensteinian era is that of the possibility of a private language. Already in 1954—that is one year after the publication of the *Philosophical Investigations*—the Joint Session of The Aristotelian Society and The Mind Association had a discussion between A. J. Ayer and Rush Rhees on the problem, with Ayer attacking and Rush Rhees defending the Wittgensteinian position. And with interludes the philosophic discussion has continued almost to today. In 1971 *The Private Language Argument* was published (Macmillan), a book containing some of the most important contributions and discussions on the topic. On the Wittgenstein side are, as just mentioned, Rush Rhees and also Norman Malcolm, both belonging to what have been called by some The Wittgenstein-Fideists.

Anthony Kenny in "Cartesian Privacy," in a book on the *Philosophical Investigations* edited by George Pitcher (1966), concludes that the argument against private language has an importance which transcends any parochial concerns of ordinary language philosophy and the disputable theories of meaning put forward in the *Philosophical Investigations.* Hector Castaneda and Judith Jarvis Thomson, however, are both critical. In a kind of summary Judith Thomson has this to say: "So the thesis we have been considering amounts to no more than a restatement of the Principle of Verification. But of course it then amounts to no less than this. Whatever can be said both for and against the one can be said both for and against the other. The only trouble is: The arguments on both sides are excessively familiar."

As so often in philosophy, so also here. It turns out that a general answer to the question about the validity of Wittgenstein's argument against a private language cannot get a straight answer. Further analysis shows that the concept of a private language can be understood in more than one way and consequently may receive more than one answer. Already Strawson in his review of the *Philosophical Investigations* (*Mind,* 1954) distinguished between what he calls a stronger thesis and a weaker thesis. The stronger thesis says that no words name sensations, while the weaker thesis says that certain conditions must be satisfied for the existence of a common language in which sensations are ascribed to those who have them. I have myself argued (cf. chapter IV of my book *Language and Philosophy,* Mouton, 1971) that the only way to describe or characterize a sensation is in terms of a public language; they can be described, recognized, or characterized in no other way. To name a sensation by help of a word (a letter, say) which in no way implies a public language is of course possible. But if it is possible to remember what the name refers to, it is due to the fact that a presupposition for naming a sensation is that one conceives of it or characterizes it by help of the public language, i.e. I may characterize it by its causes: it is a sensation which is burning, wet, etc. Which, of course, means that a so-called private name implies a public language and consequently hardly can be called a name in a private language. If no public language is implied—i.e. if the name (the letter) cannot be so characterized and therefore in the Wittgensteinian sense is a private language—there is of course no criterion for a correct or an incorrect remembrance. Let me finally add that Saul Kripke in 1982 published *Wittgenstein on Rules and Private Language.* It may well be *the* book on this topic. It is a book which is not only challenging but also challenged; it is a book which is both hailed and criticized.

When the *Tractatus* was published, it was conceived by many as a book giving support to logical positivism. Thus, Wittgenstein's concept of the Mystical, which was a concept transcending the limits of language, seems to coincide with logical positivism. Nevertheless, this conception of the *Tractatus* is mistaken. In his *Letters from Ludwig Wittgenstein* (1967) Paul Engelmann writes:

> "A whole generation of disciples was able to take Wittgenstein as a positivist, because he has something of enormous importance in common with the positivists: he draws the line between what we can speak about and what we must be silent about just as they do. The difference is only that they have nothing to be silent about. Positivism holds—and this is its essence—that what we can speak about is all that matters in life. *Whereas Wittgenstein passionately believes that all that really matters in human life is precisely what, in his view, we must be silent about.*"

148

And in a letter from Wittgenstein to Engelmann, Wittgenstein says:

> "*The book's point is an ethical one.* I once meant to include in the preface a sentence which is not in fact there now, but which I will write out for you here, because it will perhaps be a key to the work for you. What I meant to write, then, was this: My work consists of two parts: the one presented here plus all that I have *not* written. *And it is precisely this second part that is the important one.* My book draws limits to the sphere of the ethical from the inside as it were, and I am convinced that this is the ONLY rigorous way of drawing those limits."

In the same letter Wittgenstein writes: "For now I would recommend you to read the *preface* and the *conclusion* because they contain the most direct expression of the point of the book."

That which we have to be silent about, i.e. the mystical, is ethics, religion, and, in general, values. In their book *Wittgenstein's Vienna* (1973) Allan Janik and Stephen Toulmin maintain that according to the Wittgenstein of the *Tractatus* art alone can express the meaning of life. Only art can express moral truth, and only the artist can teach the things that matter most in life (p. 197). Wittgenstein's view on ethics has not been subject to the same study as has (which, of course, is obvious) that which is not relegated to mysticism. However, Wittgenstein gave a lecture on ethics to *The Heretics Society* in Cambridge, a lecture which is published in *Philosophical Review* in 1965 (cf. Theodore Redpath's article on "Wittgenstein and Ethics" in Alice Ambrose and Morris Lazerowitz, editors, *Ludwig Wittgenstein: Philosophy and Language* (1972). Another interesting article on Wittgenstein's view on mysticism is written by B. F. McGuinness, also in *Philosophical Review* (1966), in which it is argued that Wittgenstein did have a genuine mystical experience—an experience with which Wittgenstein is identifying the whole of ethics, aesthetics, and metaphysics, including the experience of feeling absolutely safe ("nothing can injure me whatever happens") and the experience of feeling guilt.

There are, of course, other problems associated with Wittgenstein's philosophy which are subject to discussion and to different interpretations. Let me, without going into discussion of them, mention two problems: (1) What should, according to Wittgenstein, count as a simple object (i.e. the constituents of atomic facts)? and (2) solipsism. Concerning the problem of what should be understood by a simple object there has been considerable disagreement. Stenius, for instance, in *Wittgenstein's Tractatus* (1960) maintains that objects include particular properties as well as relations, whereas this is denied by Elizabeth Anscombe (cf. her book *Introduction to Wittgenstein's Tractatus,* 1959, p. 27). Wittgenstein himself was rather noncommitted about it. Malcolm once asked Wittgenstein whether, when he wrote the *Tractatus,* he had ever decided upon anything as an *example* of a "simple object." Wittgenstein answered that at that time his thought had been that he was a *logician* and that it was not his business, as a logician, to try to decide whether this thing or that was a simple thing or a complex thing, that being a purely *empirical* matter (*A Memoir,* p. 86). A final answer seems not to have been given.

In *Mind* 1958 there is an interesting article by Hintikka: "On Wittgenstein's Solipsism." In this article Hintikka rejects the usual interpretation of what Wittgenstein meant by solipsism, based as it is on a mistranslation of 5.62 (instead of the translation "*the* language which I alone understand," the correct one is: "the only language that I understand"). Hintikka advocates the view that Wittgenstein was asserting that the metaphysical subject (the I of solipsism) is identical with the sum total of one's language, i.e. Wittgenstein identifies the limits of one's language with the limits of one's self. And since the limits of one's language are the limits of one's world, it follows that I am the world at the same time as this "I" is not in the world but is the limit of the world; or rather, the limit of the "I" is identical with the limit of my language. The conclusion then is that since the metaphysical subject is identical with the totality of one's language and since the limits of language are the limits of the world, it follows that the limits of the metaphysical subjects are the limits of the world.

It is interesting to compare Hintikka's interpretation with McGuinness' above-mentioned article on the mysticism of the *Tractatus.* McGuinness connects Wittgenstein's solipsism with mysticism: The insight which Wittgenstein expresses by the words "I am my world" is in part a refusal to identify oneself with one part of the world rather than another. The higher or metaphysical self feels itself identical with the whole world (*Philosophical Review,* 1966, p. 318).

Chapter V above, "Contemporary Philosophical Investigations," has the purpose of showing the influence of Wittgenstein's philosophy (in particular his later philosophy) on much of what at this book's writing could be regarded as contemporary philosophy. Needless to say the philosophic scene changes, if not by the year then at least over a quarter of a century. Although Wittgenstein's works, not least his *Nachlass,* are still studied, his philosophy taught to undergraduates and in graduate seminars, and new books on his philosophy are yet being published, the so-called ordinary language philosophy, of which Wittgenstein's later philosophy is part and parcel, no longer dominates the Anglo-American world. The Wittgenstein-inspired nonformalistic approach to philosophy has been rivaled by a movement whose most prominent member, or even instigator, is W. V. Quine of Harvard; it is a movement which vigorously has resisted the informality of linguistic philosophy as it was practiced by Wittgenstein, Ryle, and Austin, and all the philosophers inspired by them. Let me just mention Quine's *The Ways of Paradox* (1966), *From a Logical Point of View* (1953), *Word and Object* (1960), and *Ontological Relativity* (1967). During the heyday of logical positivism, political philosophy was regarded as a logical impossibility. And none of the great figures from the Wittgensteinian and ordinary-language period thought it possible to bridge the gap between the conceptual investigations they practiced and the value statements allegedly involved in political philosophy. However, due to the American philosophers John Rawls and Robert Nozick (*Theory of Justice* and *Anarchy, State and Utopia*) political philosophy, despite the alleged naturalistic fallacy, has gained (or rather regained) respect.

Western philosophy is, of course, not identical with Anglo-American philosophy. In the United States more so than in Great Britain (which seems not to be as open and hospitable to other kinds of philosophy as is the United States) philosophies such as hermeneutics, existentialism, and phenomenology are studied and researched, which means that the philosophies of Gadamer from Germany, Ricoeur and Derrida from France, Heidegger and Husserl from Germany, and Sartre from France (not to forget Kierkegaard from Denmark) are well-known in the American philosophic world.

Let it be emphasized, however, that there is no sign whatever that the Wittgensteinian philosophy is superseded by other philosophies. It is rivaled by and exists parallel to them but is not replaced by them. It is in this connection interesting to note that in a recent book by B. R. Tilghman, *But Is It Art?* (1984), the author asserts that only Wittgensteinian philosophy can dispel confusions in recent philosophy of art. In the foreword Tilghman writes: "It is the techniques of philosophical investigation that can be learned from Wittgenstein that allow the confusions in recent philosophy of art to be recognized and shown for what they are and it is some rather neglected aspects of his work that permit a better understanding of what it is that generates those philosophical missteps." Later in the foreword he says: "If this book were to have a motto, it would be Wittgenstein's description in *Philosophical Investigations* of this aspect of his philosophical method: 'What *we* do is to bring words back from their metaphysical to their everyday use'." Which is another way of stating Austin's almost truistic, but philosophically important, saying that ordinary language may not be the last word, but it is the first word.